The Thomas Factor

The Thomas Factor
Using Your Doubts to Draw Closer to God

Gary R. Habermas

BROADMAN
& HOLMAN
PUBLISHERS
Nashville, Tennessee

0-8054-1720-6

Published by Broadman & Holman Publishers, Nashville, Tennessee
Acquisitions and Development Editor: Leonard G. Goss
Page Design and Typesetting: TF Designs, Mt. Juliet, Tennessee

Dewey Decimal Classification: 220
Subject Heading: FAITH/BELIEF AND DOUBT
Library of Congress Card Catalog Number: 98-46128

Unless otherwise noted, Scripture quotations are from the Holy Bible, New
International Version, © copyright 1973, 1978, 1984.
Other versions are marked NASB, the New American Standard Bible,
© Copyright The Lockman Foundation, 1960, 1962, 1963, 1968,
1971, 1972, 1973, 1975, 1977, 1995.
NKJV, New King James Version, copyright © 1979, 1980, 1982,
Thomas Nelson, Inc., Publishers.

Quotations from William Backus and Marie Chapian,
Telling Yourself the Truth (Minneapolis: Bethany House, 1980),
are used by permission from the publisher.

Library of Congress Cataloging-in-Publication Data

Habermas, Gary R.
    The Thomas factor : using your doubts to draw closer to God / by
Gary R. Habermas.
        p. cm.
    Includes bibliographical references and index.
    ISBN 0-8054-1720-6 (pbk.)
    1. Faith. 2. Belief and doubt. I. Title.
BV4637.H25   1999
234'.23--dc21
                                                        98-46128
                                                        CIP

1 2 3 4 5 03 02 01 00 99

With love to Eileen,
In every way the perfect help meet,
Whose own love is shown in her sacrifice

Table of Contents

Introduction

Defining Religious Doubt

Our newspaper headlines tell the story. We are winning the battle against many dreaded diseases, but new ones are taking their places. Instead of physical ailments like tuberculosis, polio, typhoid fever, and malaria, we now have emotional sicknesses like anxiety disorders and various kinds of clinical depression. Many think that these latter problems may be far worse than the former, as they affect life on a broader scale, are more difficult to deal with, and are far more painful overall than their physical counterparts.

Some have called the last couple of decades the "Age of Anxiety." It seems that few descriptions provide a better idea of what this generation is about. We are worriers. We are concerned about every conceivable situation. Almost gone are the days when Russia pushing the button is our chief distress. Gone, too, is the apprehension of being drafted to fight in some foreign jungle.

But the new problems are hitting closer to home. Will I get AIDS? Can my children grow up today without coming in contact with opportunities for drugs and premarital sex? Will they make the wrong decision, given contemporary peer pressure? Or, what if some crazed individual walks into our local school or restaurant and opens fire, with me or a loved one caught in the wrong place at the wrong time? Is it true that the so-called Generation X will be the first generation to be worse than off than their parents? What does that mean?

As our culture changes, our questions have grown more philosophical, too. Are traditional values passé? Is anything always right or wrong, or does it depend on the situation? Is it even possible to find truth today (with a capital "T")? Can something be true for me and not for you? Believers today would like to think that, when it comes to our faith, we are rock-solid. Yet these kinds of questions leave many of us feeling uncomfortable. Thus, for many Christians, few things seem to be more common than questions about one's faith.

In some ways, religious doubt is not all that different from non-religious doubt; both are concerned with topics that are very dear to us. After all, why would we waste time thinking about something that doesn't really matter one way or the other? And both can involve similar thinking patterns. "What if I get AIDS?" or "What if I get fired?" are not that much different from "What if I'm not really saved?" Of course, one difference lies in the fact that religious questions concern God and the afterlife, which should be our chief concern (Matt. 22:37–38). But is this always the way it is in life? While convicting, it is just not the case that believers are always most concerned about the things of God.

Somehow it's comforting to learn that other Christians usually experience doubts about their own beliefs, too. The experts tell us that being worried by both religious and non-religious questions is simply a normal part of human life and development. In particular, religious questions of one sort or another have occurred to virtually everyone at some time.

Varieties of Doubt

Have you ever questioned the existence of God? Or that the Bible is really God's Word to us? What about difficult texts in Scripture, or the miracles that are recorded there? Do supernatural items like these seem difficult to believe as modern persons living in the twenty-first century?

What about your own faith? Have you ever wondered if you were truly a Christian, or questioned whether you said the right words when you first trusted Christ as your Savior? How much repentance is enough? What if you're pretty sure that you did the right thing, but you just want to be more sure?

How strong is your motivation to follow God? How about the strength of your faith—do you question God easily? Does your belief fluctuate, seemingly dependent on what is happening in your life or how you are doing on a particular day? Or do you think it would take a lot for you to doubt the truth of Christianity? Do you ever feel like you don't want to follow Jesus any more?

Welcome to the subject of religious doubt! It comes in several forms and is far more common than most believers think. Later we will discuss three different species of uncertainty: factual, emotional, and volitional. I characterize doubt this way both because it seems to have three different root causes, and it responds best to three sorts of solutions. But we will say more about all of this in chapters 3 and 4.

These three species of doubt can each be subdivided into the most common categories of questions. To complicate things further, the same question does not always indicate the same root cause. Frequently it is not *what* is being asked that is indicative of the problem as much as it is *why* and *how* it is being asked. This is just another reason why the topic can be a maze of problems and proposed solutions.

One familiar category concerns whether certain aspects of Christianity are true. Another is the commonly expressed need for personal assurance of salvation: How do I know if I am *really* saved? Uncertainty also comes in the form of other common questions. Why do bad things happen to those who try their best to follow the Lord? Why aren't our prayers answered? It would seem that most believers have wrestled at some time with notions such as these. For instance, Cindy was a young believer who had been taught that doubt was merely a synonym for unbelief. While struggling with her own assurance of salvation, she met Sarah, a Christian who openly asked questions about several aspects of Christianity. Cindy became confused one day when she heard Sarah comment: "There's really no difference, you know. One sort of question about God is the same as another." Startled, Cindy never asked Sarah what she meant. Were both of them doing the same thing? Privately, Cindy began to worry that perhaps neither of them was truly saved.

A Definition

In the New Testament there are at least a half dozen Greek words that describe the general condition that we have called doubt. They can also have other meanings as well, such as puzzlement or wondering. When used in the sense that is relevant for us, key meanings include uncertainty or hesitation between two positions, but there are differences. Interestingly, they are applied to believers and unbelievers alike.

For example, using the most common word for doubt *(diakrino)*, James describes the man who asks God for faith but who wavers concerning whether he thinks God will grant the request. This individual is described as being unsettled (James 1:5–8). Using the same term, Jude instructs believers to have mercy on doubters (Jude 22), who, in the context, were apparently affected by false teachers (vv. 17–23). Matthew mentions that Jesus' followers doubted *(distazo)* him on occasion (14:31; 28:17). In the first instance, Jesus identified Peter as having little faith, and asked him why he doubted. Unbelieving Jews are also described as doubting *(psuchen airo)* Jesus (John 10:24).

Other terms with similar meanings are also used. Paul describes his own condition during times of persecution as being perplexed *(aporeo),* although he said he did not despair (2 Cor. 4:8). Jesus uses still another word *(meteorizo)* when warning His listeners about anxious worry (Luke 12:29). Such words regularly indicate a state of vacillation or questioning, even of anxiety, despair, or unbelief. There is also much variety in the use of these terms, depending on the context. So doubt covers a fairly wide range of possible states of mind, with some diversity regarding the particular situation. It can tend in the direction of unbelief, but it is most commonly used of true believers who lack assurance. We will see a number of examples in the next chapter.

It is instructive that there are no hard lines of distinction here, either. Both believers and unbelievers doubted Jesus, for example. Both Jesus and James scolded those with weak faith. So we are not to take these states of mind lightly. Neither are we free to make comments implying that doubt is always a positive state, or that it isn't potentially dangerous. We do need to deal with it. But the other side needs to be noted, too. Not all states of doubt are created equal, largely because doubt doesn't always say the same thing. Even in Scripture, it is not always rebuked. Sometimes it even preceded victory.

For the purposes of this book, we will define doubt as the lack of certainty about the truthfulness of Christianity, one's own faith, or how it applies to real life situations. Except for occasional comments, especially in the next chapter, only believers will be addressed.

A Personal Quest

I am not a psychologist. This is not a psychology text. I have come to these issues from an intensely personal perspective. I questioned my own faith for ten straight years, then off and on for perhaps another five years. It got to the point where matters of faith were the predominant thoughts in my mind. They were the last thing I contemplated when I crawled, exhausted, into bed. They were the first thoughts to greet me when I rose in the morning: "Where did I leave off the night before?" I hated (this may still not be a strong enough term!) my doubts with every fiber of my being. I wondered if I would ever overcome them, or if it was even possible to do so.

My questions pushed me into a personal quest. The area of apologetics (defending the faith) quickly became my favorite topic of study. I told myself repeatedly that a good dose of evidences would solve all of my doubts. What I found out, many years and thousands of books later, was that while having a firm foundation was helpful as a base, and certainly addressed certain sorts of questions, it was impotent against other forms of doubt. That was a shock.

Another important personal discovery came during the time when I pastored a couple of churches, when I realized that some kinds of uncertainty were also the most common questions I heard in pastoral counseling. After finishing my doctorate, I began teaching college and the lesson continued. Probably because they discovered a "fellow doubter," as one student proclaimed, I started to attract others who were similarly plagued. Soon more and more people called. Surprisingly, they included both unbelievers as well as believers. It seemed that this was a subject that affected most people at some time in their lives.

Early in the process, I began to take notes. I kept a card file on each searching person, including their specific type of question, how it originated, and what approach seemed most helpful. Each time, I sought to uncover and record a specific lesson. Eventually, the numbers mounted to over one hundred hurting persons. I realized doubt was much more multifaceted than I had ever imagined, and the same solution that helped one person was frequently not what the next person needed.

I was intrigued by these differences, and tried to think through each aspect very carefully. Why were there different starting points? Why did doubt seem so emotionally based on some occasions but not on others? Why did some doubters barely seem to care that they were bothered? Some questions appeared to be rather simple, while others were compounded by multiple factors. Surprisingly, the differences could not all be explained on the basis of the various personalities involved.

Theory very quickly melded to practice. It had to be or I would soon have nothing to say to those who sought advice. It was one thing to lecture on the subject. It was another to go through it myself, and then something else again to try to counsel others. Like an umbrella, theory needed to be large enough and real enough that it could shield those who sat under it.

Purpose

This book is for Christians who doubt. It is addressed to all those who are uneasy about their faith, but especially those whose doubts take on an emotional form. What happens when our faith somehow gets mixed up with our anxieties? What do I do when worries about life involve my most personal and cherished beliefs? Why must faith seem so difficult? Doesn't God care that I am really hurting? If I have doubts, does that mean that I am not really saved? At the final judgment, will Jesus say he never knew me? Did the saints in the Bible fight these sorts of battles?

Thus, the primary purpose of this book is to address this emotional side of faith as a symptom of the larger problem of worry. How do I overcome emotional hurdles associated with my beliefs? How do I keep believing what I accept as true? Why can't I just rest in my faith and enjoy the Christian life? Or conversely, when I'm worried, why can't the solution be an easy one? Why can't I just take two aspirins and go to bed? Why must it all be so complicated?

This book is a popular attempt to share what I found over the years of personal experience, study, lecturing, and sharing. It is not a technical text. It is written in a popular style with the hope that the lack of specialized jargon and references to dozens of other books will help those who struggle. For those who are interested, an earlier, different volume, contained in the bibliography, provides more of the theory involved.

Achieving our goal will involve accomplishing two major purposes. Initially, we will survey the subject of doubt in the first three chapters. Few topics involve so much confusion and so many mistaken beliefs. Frequently, the truth is *precisely the opposite* of what we have been taught, and pain often results from trying to reconcile contradictory advice. That's one reason why an overview is so important. Like a medical problem, unless the dilemma is correctly identified, it may never be properly treated. We will also zero in on the three major species of doubt, concentrating on emotional doubt in particular. It is probably the most common, as well as the most painful, variety. It demands a remedy.

In the second half of the book, the central theme will be to address the more obvious side effects of emotional doubt and provide some hints for its successful treatment. Achieving a workable solution is important in order to deal with the contorted thinking, as well as the amount of pain, that is sometimes involved. While emotional doubt can still produce many positive consequences, it frequently causes situations that demand attention. We want to profile its nature, as well as provide some hints for dealing with this common modern phenomenon.

Along the way, I will use many illustrations and stories about people who have dealt with religious uncertainty. In no case is a specific person being discussed, to avoid any identification. Rather, I have changed names, significant circumstances, and other details, or used composites that reproduce typical questions that I have heard in twenty years of listening and lecturing on this topic. In this way I hope that you, the reader, will glean from others' experiences.

Both Believers
and Unbelievers

A Christian friend of mine once had dinner with a world-renowned atheist. During the meal, my friend asked the philosopher if he had ever doubted his atheism. To his surprise, the atheist responded: "Oh yes, I question the truth of my atheism all the time."

Does this episode surprise you, too? Have you ever wondered why it is sometimes so difficult to believe? Have you ever thought that non-Christians have it so much easier because they have nothing to doubt (or to believe, either)? How about an even tougher question: Have you ever scared yourself with the fleeting thought that it might even be preferable to be a nonbeliever, believing this would uncomplicate your life?

We have said that the subject of doubt involves many twists and turns, including some that are very much unexpected. Some Christians might think that doubt only affects believers, while others may conclude that only non-Christians should fit this description. Yet, both are described in the New Testament by the term.

It seems to me, after talking to doubters for more than twenty years, that there are strong reasons to think that virtually all Christians raise questions about God or their faith at some time. Only on two occasions have I ever heard a Christian deny that this was the case in their personal lives. One occasion was when I heard a lecture given by a nationally known professor and author of dozens of books. (He had also written an article on the subject of doubt.) He insisted that he had never even once questioned God or his faith. The statement was made so firmly, and seemingly with full knowledge of the nature of doubt, that it haunted me for a few years. Later, the professor and I were alone for a meal and I brought the subject up again.

"Oh, you misunderstood me," he explained. "I was only referring to not having certain types of questions. I often wonder why God does things the way he does, when it appears to me it should happen some other way!" I learned an important lesson that day. Once again, this topic defied expectations.

The other time someone told me they had never doubted, I had the opportunity to pursue the comment on the spot. The individual was the child of missionary parents and had been raised on the mission field. After I spoke to her and to someone who knew her very well, the final response was that she had truly never asked any questions of doubt. While I am still somewhat skeptical of this assertion, even to this day, it is one more reason not to be overly dogmatic when speaking about what *must always* be the case.

Old Testament Examples

Was it true in biblical times that believers frequently experienced doubt of one sort or another? Did our heroes of the faith likewise struggle with some of these same issues? What about unbelievers—do they ever question their opinions?

Throughout the Bible there are literally dozens of verses where true believers express their uncertainties, often in very strong terms. Several examples may be helpful in illustrating both points that we have already made, as well as in providing grounds for further lessons.

The Case of Job. The book of Job presents enough material for an entire chapter (or book) on the expression of doubts concerning God, so we must be brief here. The basic story is a familiar one. God allowed Satan to test Job, a righteous man and God's servant, to see if his faith was strong (1:6–12; 2:1–7). His sons and daughters were killed in a tornado-like storm; most of his servants and livestock were killed by robbers; Job himself was in pain, inflicted over his entire body by sores (1:13–19; 2:7–8). Even his wife suggested that he give up his integrity, curse God, and then die (2:9). At first, Job remained firm: he accepted the calamity and praised God. He rejected his wife's advice and refused to sin (1:21–22; 2:10–11).

But during the middle chapters of the book, in the portions that seem seldom to be read and digested, Job posed heartrending questions about his suffering, even blaming God for it. He seemed to gain momentum as he went. He expressed what today would be called a death wish, stating his preference to have died in childbirth (3:11; 10:18–19). Then he requested that God slay him (6:8–9). He charged God with oppressing him, while approving the actions of the wicked (10:3). Further, he said that God was watching him, just waiting for him to make a mistake (10:14). Then he demanded that God just leave him alone (10:20–21) and stop trying to frighten him (13:21). After all, he thought that God had destroyed any hope that he might have (14:19).

In a major subtheme, Job asserted his prerogative to complain (7:11) and even challenged God to a debate (13:3). He thought he had a right to state his case, wanting to offer his arguments in order to justify himself (23:4–5), and have God reply (13:22)! As far as Job was concerned, God had not spoken to him; he remained silent (19:7; 30:20) and denied the man the justice he felt he was due (27:2).

Interestingly, Job was not punished for all of these accusations against the God of the universe, as far as we know. Although he had sinned (34:37), he also repented (40:3–5; 42:6). God honored his response and blessed him with far more than he had before disaster befell him (42:10–17).

Through all of this, Job learned some tremendous lessons that were exceptionally valuable. Although he never found out why he suffered, he learned a greater truth: *God was trustworthy in those things that he did not understand* (42:1–6). This information ultimately made him impregnable to the dilemma of why he suffered as he had. As long as he knew what he did about the nature of God, he also knew that there was a reason for the suffering, *even if he did not know what it was*. What greater lesson was there for him to learn? And, it came at least partially through the doubt that he experienced.

The Case of Abraham. Next to Job, the best case of doubt in the Old Testament comes, paradoxically, from Abraham, whom Scripture calls a man of faith. In fact, perhaps no man in the Old Testament is better known for this attribute. Certainly his trust in God did not come easily, and his struggles can assist us thousands of years later. Like Job, the general overview of his story is well known. God spoke to Abraham (who was still called Abram) and told him to take his family and move from his homeland, traveling westward to the land of Canaan. He was given a special promise: a great nation would come from him in this new country and, through it, all the peoples of the earth would be blessed (Gen. 12:1–3). Abraham and his family obeyed the Lord and, after several incidents, settled in the land of Canaan, which God had given to him. He and his wife Sarah (initially called Sarai) lived together for many years and later died in that country. God greatly blessed them, and Abraham became the father of the Israelites through his son, Isaac, and his grandson, Jacob.

Many centuries later, the book of Hebrews showcased the life of Abraham. For the Jews, he was the Most Valuable Player from a long history of stars, and all of his accomplishments were won by faith in the God who called him. Abraham responded to God's call and migrated to Canaan, even though he did not know where he was going (Heb. 11:8–10). Later, he believed God's promise that he and Sarah would have a child, even though there were two huge roadblocks: both of them were well beyond the childbearing years, and Sarah was barren. But because Abraham believed that God was trustworthy, he became the father of a great nation (11:11–12).

Further, after his son Isaac was born, Abraham was willing to sacrifice the child of promise, again because he believed God and trusted him. He believed God would raise Isaac from the dead, if necessary (11:17–19). James captured the chief idea like this: Abraham lived his life by faith, and God honored and blessed him (James 2:21–24).

At this point, some might wonder what's the point of all of this? The history lesson is nice, you might think, but how can we really relate to Abraham? That's tougher than trying to hit a home run just because we know that Babe Ruth was able to hit so many! And didn't Abraham have advantages that we, frankly, never have? Didn't God speak directly to him? Couldn't Abraham continue to talk directly to God whenever he wanted to do so? Didn't God always respond? Those were simply far different times from today, right? It cannot be the same for us.

But if we go back and examine the texts more closely, we may find something quite different. What if Abraham also struggled with the question of God's silence? What if he didn't hear from God on a regular basis? What if he, too, needed assurance that God was at work in his life?

For instance, at the close of Genesis 16, Abraham was 86 years old (16:16). As far as we are told, God didn't speak to him until 13 years later, when Abraham was 99 (Gen. 17:1)! We cannot be dogmatic here, but it is at least possible that God did not communicate with Abraham over a long period of years. From the other chapters, it doesn't appear that God conversed with Abraham on a weekly or even a yearly basis during the rest of his life, either. There may have been sizable gaps. Wouldn't most Christians even today say that God had communicated with them more than once in the last thirteen years?

Yes, Abraham was certainly a man of great faith. And God did speak to him, although perhaps not anywhere near as often as what we might have thought. But this did not keep Abraham from asking God for the assurance of his promises, i.e., how could he be certain that Canaan would be given to him (Gen. 15:8)? The Lord allowed him to know this truth by the use of a supernatural manifestation in order to make a covenant with Abraham (15:13–21). Faith does not exclude asking good questions and receiving good answers!

Yet, all of this—God's call and supernatural revelation—did not keep Abraham from undergoing several troublesome moments. Like Job, Abraham also struggled with his faith. On two occasions, he purposely concealed the identity of Sarah in order to save his own life (12:10–20; 20:1–18). But we have to answer a tough question here: if Abraham really believed that God would raise up a great nation from him, why should he be so fearful for his life, as the texts tell us (12:12–13; 20:11)? Then when Sarah still hadn't conceived the promised child, she was able to convince Abraham to bear a son (Ishmael) by her servant Hagar, in spite of God's promises (16:1–16). It seemed she wanted to help God along. Yet, Abraham agreed with her. Then when the Lord repeated the promise that Sarah would bear a child, Abraham literally laughed at God (17:15–17), as Sarah did later (18:10–15)! Where was that faith that made him so famous?

It would be wrong to malign Abraham's faith. These episodes were spread over twenty-five years (cf. Gen. 12:4 with 21:5), providing many chances for doubt. No one has lived a perfectly consistent life except our Lord Jesus Christ. Overall, Abraham acted in faith, and never allowed unbelief to master him. In fact, we should understand Abraham very well. Haven't we ever acted similarly, perhaps by attempting to rationalize our faith and help God along? We say, "Maybe what God really meant was. . . ." We can understand Abraham and be encouraged by his actions precisely because, just like us, he failed several times. We can relate to that!

How did Abraham overcome his doubts regarding God's promises? Paul used Abraham as his example, in spite of these momentary lapses in faith. When he could have walked away and ignored God's call, Abraham chose to believe instead. When he was promised a child, he trusted God, even though all the medical data opposed it. Rather than give up or cease to believe, Abraham's faith was actually strengthened (Rom. 4:18–25). So here we find one of his secrets: Abraham not only exercised his faith, but it *grew* as he trusted God more and more, one step at a time, even after several failures.

Imagine having a faith that grows when life's pressures are at their peak! Yet that was Abraham's experience. Like Job, the primary reason for this is that he concluded that God was trustworthy. What he already knew about God was enough to trust him in unknown areas (Rom. 4:20–21). New steps were taken, based on what had already transpired. Abraham trusted God and was strengthened even during the toughest of times.

Other Texts. Another Old Testament book that contains open, honest questioning by believers is the Psalms. Like Job, one theme is also that of evil. Several psalms charge God with allowing the wicked to enjoy life (like 74:1), while the godly gain nothing but adversity (73:12–14). God, it seems, defends and shows favoritism towards the wicked (Ps. 82:2). This sort of bewilderment is found elsewhere, too, like Jeremiah 12:1–2 and 15:18.

A second theme which concerned Job and Abraham, as well as the psalmists, was God's silence. David complained that his prayers went unanswered (35:13–14). Then, after sinning, he cried out to God to restore the assurance of his salvation, like he had once experienced it (Ps. 51:8–12). Other psalmists declared that they had not heard from

God in quite a while (74:9). This idea also occurs in other Old Testament books, like Lamentations 3:44 and Isaiah 57:11; 59:2. In Daniel 10:10–14, one of the prophet's prayer requests was delayed for three weeks by an attack on God's angelic messenger from what appears to be demonic forces!

Perhaps the strongest complaints about God from a single text occur in Psalm 44. Here, the writer, in very strong language, rebukes God for not fulfilling His promises even though Israel had done nothing wrong (44:17–26; cf. 89:38–39). Then, in a simply startling statement, the writer goes on to blame the God of the universe for sleeping on the job (44:23)!

One last example of God's silence during Old Testament times occurs at the close of the prophet Malachi's ministry. Between then and the birth of Jesus Christ, about four hundred years passed without a canonical prophet or book. Of course, this does not mean that God was not at work. But like the comment in Psalm 74:9, many may have wondered how long it would be before the Lord officially spoke. Was God angry with his people? Had he cast them away and rejected them? Was he done giving the inspired Scriptures? Would no prophet come forward and speak for him? When would the silence end?

Another verse in the book of Psalms may give a little hint. Just as the darkest of nights is still followed by a new sunrise (Ps. 30:5), so the Jewish "dark ages" would officially end when the Messiah entered human history, to die and rise in order to offer redemption to the world. God's profound silence was broken by the most splendid turn of events in all of history.

New Testament Examples

Although much shorter and with significantly less narrative than its counterpart, the New Testament also presents some major cases of doubting believers, from which we can learn.

In a startling but frequently overlooked text, John the Baptist, while in prison, sent two of his disciples to Jesus with a question or two: was Jesus the Messiah or should John be looking for someone else (Matt. 11:1–11; Luke 7:18–30)? On the surface at least, doesn't this seem like an unnerving question to ask the Son of God? It's not just the question itself that's so staggering. If it had come from someone in the crowd, it would probably be dismissed by many readers as being from someone who lacked faith. What turns it into such a bombshell is that it comes from John the Baptist, God's chosen forerunner for Jesus, predicted in the Old Testament (Isa. 40:1–3). Was John in danger of throwing his faith overboard?

First, let's note Jesus' immediate response. He didn't react in a vindictive fashion, such as by telling John to shape up, or to live up to his reputation, or by quoting verses to him and reminding him of his special position as the chosen herald of the Lord's coming. Neither did he, as some Christians would suggest, ignore evidences that might address John's need. Rather, he cured a number of suffering people right there in front of the two messengers, and then instructed them to go tell John what they just witnessed. Apparently, there was some relevance between Jesus' healing miracles and his messiahship, which would serve to strengthen John's faith. That is a lesson in itself.

But the story doesn't stop there; notice a second development. As the two visitors left, Jesus addressed the crowd concerning John. He asked them if, when they went out in the wilderness to see John, they had expected to see someone who was easily shaken by the wind (somewhat reminiscent of James' warning about weak faith in James 1:6–8), or did they see a weakling in soft, comfortable clothes? Then Jesus told his listeners that John not only was a prophet, but he proclaimed that no greater man had ever been born! What makes this statement even more incredible is that John hadn't yet received Jesus' message. That is to say, Jesus was complimenting John *while he was still doubting!*

Though there was no rebuke for John's lack of faith, Jesus did instruct the prophet not to be offended because of him (Matt. 11:6; Luke 7:23). I take this to be like an encouragement we might give someone today: "Hang in there. Don't give up!"

I hesitate to mention another case from the Gospels, for fear there may be some misunderstanding. What do we do with Jesus' distress in the Garden of Gethsemane? We are told that his mental suffering was so intense that he sweated drops of blood (Luke 22:39–44; cf. Mark 14:33–36; Matt. 26:36–43). This signals an extraordinary amount of strain as Jesus prayed to His father that the coming events be bypassed, but only if it was God's will. Certainly the portion of the prayer relating to God's will was accomplished, but what about Jesus' first request?

It is very difficult to address this incident. Taking the texts in a straightforward manner, Jesus undeniably suffered emotional anguish, brought about by the questions that he faced. We may agree that here is an example where Jesus encountered some of the same problems we face, yet without sinning (Heb. 4:15). We might even say this was one of the times where Jesus learned obedience by his suffering (Heb. 5:8). This is why believers today can identify with him: he personally experienced the reality of emotional pain.

The case of "Doubting Thomas" (John 20:24–29) is probably the best known example of uncertainty in the New Testament. Thomas wanted to see the risen Jesus with his own eyes before he would believe. Although Jesus did provide the requested evidence, he also issued a mild rebuke to the disciple. It would have been better if Thomas had believed (without seeing) the testimony of the other disciples, who reported to him that they had seen Jesus alive (John 20:29). Once again, Jesus does not shy away from using evidence to answer doubts, but he didn't think that Thomas's desire—a personal appearance—was the best option.

Another example of doubt is found in one of Paul's letters, where he specifically tells us that he prayed on three occasions concerning the removal of an apparent physical problem. Some think that he had problems with his eyes, others, recurring bouts of malaria. After all, didn't he need to be healthy in order to minister? But Paul was not answered as he had hoped (2 Cor. 12:7–10). He learned what Jesus already knew, that God's will was to be preferred above one's own.

What about unbelievers? In more than one place, we are told that they asked questions, too. Jesus rebuked those who wanted proof that he was from God (Matt. 12:38–45; 16:1–4). He offered his miracles to other Jews who accused him of making them doubt by not telling them who he was, but they refused to believe anyway (John 10:24–26, 37–39). He even healed a boy whose father confessed: "I do believe; help me overcome my unbelief" (Mark 9:24). And Paul says that Jews frequently asked for signs (1 Cor. 1:22–23).

Lessons

Before we return to our task of deciphering the maze of Christian doubt, we need to pause long enough to point out some lessons that come strictly from the texts that we have just discussed. We can learn from the experiences of believers who have traveled this path before us.

(1) As we have already said in our opening discussion, doubt is multifaceted. This should be even more obvious after a brief survey of its expression in the Scriptures. The presence of evil and the issue of God's silence are two of the most common problem areas. Assurance is another key issue, whether concerning the certainty of truth or of one's own salvation. Other saints struggle with God's guidance and promises, especially as they impacted their expectations. It is helpful just to see some of the various manifestations of this widespread phenomena.

(2) Some doubt is rebuked, as in the cases of Job and Thomas. And God honors repentance, as with Job. But not all doubt is reprimanded, and not all questions are deemed to be sinful (Abraham, Paul). Neither

does doubt keep a person from being complimented for his righteousness (John the Baptist). But what about especially strong expressions of doubt that are uncensored, like Psalm 44? It seems that the Holy Spirit allowed the honest expression of feelings by true believers, even when it was not always appropriate or true. But this is certainly not an excuse for us to try the same thing, or to blame God for whatever happens to us. Honest, unpremeditated questions are one thing; constant preoccupation with strong statements that question God's character may indicate something else altogether.

(3) Believers like Job, Abraham, and Paul grew during their times of doubt, even when their faith underwent the harshest attacks. Today, too, while uncertainty can have negative results to be avoided, it can also help us to learn some indispensable lessons. Perhaps the main issue here is what Christians do about their struggles. To whom do we turn, and what is our attitude towards what is happening? What applications do we make?

(4) One lesson is so crucial that it deserves mention by itself. Believers like Job and Abraham learned that God could, indeed, be trusted, even when they couldn't figure everything out. They discovered that they already knew enough about God in order to have confidence in him in those things that they didn't know or understand.

Sometimes we, too, just need to trust him more, in light of this truth. Few lessons are more valuable for us today, since we know far more than did these Old Testament saints. Just to be sure that Jesus Christ died on the cross for our sins and rose again from the dead should make us willing to trust him in times when we don't understand why things are happening as they are. After all, we don't have to figure out everything in order to know that these truths ensure heaven, where we will ultimately understand all things! This approach needs to be generously applied to all of our struggles.

(5) Many times in Scripture, doubt is simply expressed without any remedy being provided. But when relief does come, we get some hints

about what helped to bring the comfort. While the use of evidences is not the remedy in most cases, it is certainly one of the most frequent means of treating doubt and was employed when appropriate. Abraham received a sign of God's blessing, while John the Baptist's disciples presumably told him about Jesus' miracles. The risen Jesus appeared to Thomas. Other methods were also helpful. The psalmists suggested praise even when their circumstances hadn't changed yet (Ps. 35:27–28; 89:52). Another recommendation was to remember and proclaim what God had already done in history (Ps. 105–106; Lam. 3:21–26). Job found comfort through dialogue. David and Paul discovered consolation in God's truth.

(6) Concerning unbelievers, it appears that Jesus treated differently the various requests he received for a sign. John the Baptist wasn't rebuked, while Thomas received a mild admonishment, but neither was he refused. On the other hand, the unbelieving Jews were strongly chided after they demanded a sign, although they were told that Jesus' resurrection should be enough (Matt. 12:39; 16:4). What was the distinction? Why were some shown miracles and others were denied? It seems that Jesus differentiated between his listeners, based on the state of their hearts. The strongest reprimand was reserved for those who were closed to his work, no matter what he did.

But it cannot be said that he reserved his miracles for believers only. On one occasion he healed a man's son after the former's confession of partial unbelief (Mark 9:24). It could even be argued that Thomas was not a Christian when he demanded to see the resurrected Jesus. Not only did Thomas refuse to believe the resurrection until Jesus appeared to him (and this event is an indispensable part of the gospel—1 Cor. 15:3–4), but Jesus said that Thomas believed *only after* seeing him (John 20:25, 29). Lastly, as we mentioned, Jesus said that the sign of the resurrection would still be given even to the staunchest of skeptics (Matt. 12:39; 16:4). Many of his works were done before crowds, presumably including unbelievers.

A more contemporary example is provided by C. S. Lewis, who was an ardent atheist during his early teaching at Oxford University. And, he confessed, he sometimes experienced doubts about his faith even after he became a Christian. But, he added, in the days when he was an atheist, there were times when the Christian faith appeared to be "terribly probable." No matter what you believe, Lewis says, you will doubt at some time. The more important matter is, how will you deal with the doubt when it comes? (*Mere Christianity*, Macmillan, 1952, pp. 123–24).

(7) These statements by Lewis provide the opportunity for a reassessment of some of our earlier comments. Sure, Christians can have rough times. God has certainly not promised us anything different. Yet, how would it be to walk a mile in the atheist's shoes? How would you like to be an unbeliever and secretly fear that Christianity may, in fact, be true? How long would it take you to move from that thought to the petrifying realization that hell might just await you?

In the passages we looked at, Scripture plainly reveals the presence of doubt in the lives of believers and unbelievers alike. People doubt for a very basic reason—all of us are human beings and we share a sin nature. This is the *root* cause of our uncertainty. In other words, our sinful human nature is the state from which all of this questioning springs. However, this is *not* to say that all doubt is necessarily sin.

Randy was a believer who kept his questions concerning his faith to himself. But the more he did so, the more they bothered him. He never heard the subject of doubt discussed in sermons, so he concluded that very few Christians struggle with it. One day when it seemed to nag him a little more than usual, he took a chance and dropped some hints to a spiritually knowledgeable friend. It would be an understatement to say that Randy was surprised to find that religious doubt was a very normal problem, and that even his friend was not exempt! Further, when his friend turned to one Scripture passage after another to illustrate his point, Randy grew more and more relieved. Just to know that other Christians struggle with this subject seemed to relieve much of his concern.

We conclude that religious doubt is very common and affects almost everyone at some time. It is not necessarily sin, nor must it be the opposite of faith. It can even produce some good results. But it can also lead to serious situations that need to be treated. Along the way, however, there are many misconceptions concerning this topic. It just seems that doubt has an image problem!

2

Common Myths

Have you ever been sick and purchased the medicine that you thought you needed, only to discover that you did not get any better? Perhaps after another trip to your physician, you got different medicine, and began to feel well. Obviously, the key was getting the proper diagnosis and treatment. If either is incorrect, one may never get rid of the symptoms.

So it is with doubt, too. Getting the correct diagnosis and remedy are crucial to overcoming the problem and finding relief. While we will deal more directly with these two topics in coming chapters, we will begin by noting many of the common myths concerning religious uncertainty. As in our previous story, beginning with the correct information provides a much more likely chance of curing the hurt. Few topics are subject to more misconceptions than that of doubt. Since starting with truth is critical, we want to continue laying a foundation on which to build as we move along. Here are a few examples of how misbeliefs about religious uncertainty create problems.

Dave reasoned that since doubt was the opposite of faith, his continued questions must mean that he had committed the unpardonable sin. While he longed more than anything for forgiveness and fellowship with God, he believed he had forfeited both by his objections. This conclusion caused him incredible amounts of emotional torment, including thinking that he would never be able to find what he wanted most of all in life: lasting assurance and peace.

Alicia thought that biblical characters never doubted because God was in constant and regular contact with them, unlike today. But she also knew that she and many of her believing friends *did* have questions about Christianity, including the feeling that the Creator had been silent towards them. Her incorrect beliefs led her to draw faulty conclusions about the nature of God. These, in turn, were detrimental to her spiritual growth.

John was an unbeliever, who thought that doubts generally occurred only to conservative Christians as a direct result of their strict social standards. It seemed that all he ever heard from them was, "Do this . . . don't do that." This largely accounted for his decision to avoid orthodox Christianity in all of its forms, including those persons who believed it for fear that he might become "contaminated."

Each of these individuals suffered in one way or another due to believing and acting upon false information. You may recall my own testimony. I can understand these sorts of mistakes because I also was badly misinformed, even though I professed a long-standing interest in the topic. Let's investigate some of these misbeliefs that one frequently hears regarding the subject of religious uncertainty. Some of our assertions will make use of the Scripture passages that we viewed in the last chapter.

Doubt never occurs to heroes in the Bible. We devoted the last chapter to showing that there are plenty of reasons to reject this contention. But because it is commonly thought to be true, we mention it again. Job, Abraham, David, other writers of the inspired Psalms, Jeremiah, John the Baptist, the apostle Paul, and others are all witnesses against this charge. Although all these men were biblical superheroes, they were also human beings and sinners. They followed God, but they struggled at times, too. This is one reason why they can be such examples for us, even today. It would seem that anyone who takes the Bible at face value would have to agree.

We also saw that these biblical champions grappled with matters like the presence of evil in the world and the silence of God. Contrary to Alicia's belief in the story above, they were not in unbroken communication with God. They had many of the same questions as we do in our generation. Alicia needs to correct her false impressions so that she does not compromise her view of God's nature and stunt her spiritual growth.

Doubt only affects Christians, but never atheists or other unbelievers. We have also addressed this assertion in some detail and found it to be incorrect. Certain unbelievers in Scripture were open to God, while others hardened their hearts against him. Some didn't believe even after they saw Jesus' miracles. Hence, Jesus responded differently to each of them.

Not only do we have the witness of Scripture that non-Christians can live in a state of doubt, but contemporary writers like C. S. Lewis have given their own testimonies to this fact, as well. Obviously biblical heroes and doubters along with modern-day skeptics all have something in common: they are all human beings, existing in a fallen, sinful state. This is the *root cause* for the problem we have been discussing and the chief reason why doubt is not a respecter of persons.

One related charge is that only *conservative* Christians are regular doubters, like John's complaint in our story above. Granted, the excessive following of rules can, without question, contribute to uncertainty at any of several levels. But we have already seen that far more than just conservatives are involved; people from all walks of life question their religious beliefs. So John's complaint was itself too selective in not recognizing the pervasiveness of doubt. He had rejected orthodox Christianity for illegitimate reasons.

Doubt is relatively rare. Admittedly, just because both believers and unbelievers experience religious uncertainty, this does not mean that it is common. Neither does the Bible appear to answer this question, except by implication. Even so, since this phenomenon is so widespread throughout Scripture, involving so many persons, the thought that it is at least fairly frequent would seem to follow. One might offer two further biblical points as well. That so many of those who experienced doubt were spiritual giants only adds to the contention that it probably happens to many who are not so spiritually attuned. Further, since everyone shares a common human, sinful thread, we might even expect that this experience would be a regular occurrence.

To these biblical considerations, we can add countless testimonies from people today—believers and unbelievers alike. I have already said that dozens of my own interviews have led me to suspect that it is extremely common if not universal. Of course, I don't claim scientific data for this conclusion.

Doubt is the opposite of faith; it is actually unbelief. This is another protest that we have already addressed. While doubt *can* tend in the direction of unbelief, and while it *is* expressed by unbelievers as well as believers, this is certainly not the case with the majority of examples in the Bible. Most of the time, it is believers themselves who ask the questions and pose the problems. (Of course, Scripture chiefly addresses believers, so we cannot use this to say that more Christians than non-Christians doubt.) In our definition, we saw that doubt more frequently contains the idea of being caught in between two positions. There is a Greek noun for belief *(pistis)* and another one for unbelief *(apistia)*. Doubt is neither: it more commonly expresses ideas such as perplexity, worry, uncertainty, or perhaps weak faith.

To see if doubt is really unbelief, recalling a few of the instances that we have already looked at might be helpful. In the Old Testament, Job was not only a righteous servant of God when Satan began to tempt him, but he was vindicated in the end, too. Never was he addressed by God as an unbeliever. This was even more the case with Abraham, the man of faith. To call his questions the result of unbelief is simply to miss the point of his entire story. While David sinned, he was also one of the chief examples of a man of God. Sure, he struggled with his faith on occasion, but he was unquestionably a believer.

In the New Testament, we dare not call John the Baptist's doubt unbelief, or we would be contradicting our Lord's assertion that he was the most (godly) righteous man ever born of a woman. Neither could it be properly claimed that Paul's unanswered prayers were due to unbelief. And what about Jesus' emotional struggles in the Garden of Gethsemane? It seems that we would have to do some fast talking here!

Therefore we conclude that doubt can be negative and does, on occasion, incline towards unbelief. However its normal biblical use is to describe believers who struggle with various aspects of their faith. We even have cases where strong charges are made against God, but where the individual is definitely a believer.

Doubt always indicates that something serious is wrong; perhaps it is even the unpardonable sin. This is the first of several charges that, while not totally wrong, are half-truths. But since part of the notion is correct, sometimes half-truths are more hurtful than total misbeliefs.

We might begin here by noting a certain amount of general agreement with the assertion. Yes, the presence of ongoing doubt that is more than a passing mood or momentary pressure may well be a signal that something is wrong. That is why this book is being written. It doesn't follow, however, that this "wrongness" is something that is necessarily spiritual (although it certainly may be). It could mean the presence of medical or emotional factors that need to be dealt with. But while emotional doubt, in particular, can be very painful, it doesn't always follow that the level of hurt indicates that something is terribly wrong spiritually. This frequent incommensurability between pain and serious spiritual "illness" is one of the many false alarms about doubt.

In contrast, the notion about the unpardonable sin would appear to be quite mistaken. I believe commentators would agree that this condition is an ongoing state of mind, not the result of a momentary lapse. It generally proceeds from a settled attitude that rejects (and *continues* to reject) God, not from a brief, angry outburst(s). This is not to overlook the latter, because it can be serious, too; but only to say that it doesn't seem to qualify as a unforgivable condition. Most scholars would say that Dave's attitude shows that he certainly didn't commit the unpardonable sin. His desire for repentance and his longing for God, along with the fact that questions about God do not automatically cause one to enact this dreaded sin, are the best indications of this.

Further, if normal doubts qualify one for the unforgivable sin, then why was it not committed by the writer in Psalm 44? Don't many of the other Psalms that challenge God end in thanksgiving and praise without any indication that the authors are unbelievers? Wouldn't Job's thirty chapters of constant and even excessive challenges against God show that he was in an unforgivable state? Yet God accepts his repentance at the end of the book! How many strikes does Abraham get before he would have been called out? Could he ever be known as the man of faith and figure so prominently in Hebrews 11 if this objection were true? When David committed the double sin of murder and adultery with Bathsheba, causing his questions of assurance, why could he later repent, recover, and become a man after God's heart? What about John the Baptist's seeming readiness to look for another "messiah"? If he had crossed the line to the unpardonable sin, could Jesus have paid him the tremendous compliment that he did?

It would seem, then, that the biblical material, over and over again, suggests that we should reject this charge against religious uncertainty or doubt. To be sure, the unpardonable sin is real and to be avoided at all costs. But raising questions such as those we have been considering does not appear to qualify.

Doubt shouldn't be admitted or discussed since it is basically a character flaw. In a sense, religious uncertainty *does* come from a character flaw—our fallen nature, resulting from our sin! But it doesn't follow that it is therefore something that should be shut up and kept away from others, like a rabid dog, or some highly contagious disease. Here we have another half-truth. Questioning one's faith can be infectious. But so can finding biblical, godly solutions. In fact, this is precisely one of the reasons why it *should* be both admitted and discussed. This is a subject where public examination can be one of the surest ways to find relief and healing.

There is another sense in which doubt is a character trait. It most frequently follows personality types, as we will see later, making it important that we recognize our personal tendencies and understand ahead of time where they very well might lead. Frequently, all we may need to say to ourselves during a period of religious vacillation is: "That's just me again! Calm down." Recognizing and reading our predispositions is an indispensable part of handling doubt. But this is a topic that comes later.

Doubt is usually factual in nature, and is always satisfied by studying the evidence. I said earlier that this was my initial thought back in my early days of doubting. This conviction lasted through years of study. But I found myself wondering on many occasions why a careful marshaling of the facts, even in cases where the factual basis was overwhelmingly strong, did not always calm the uncertainty. This was especially so when the questioning took on emotional or volitional dimensions. It was immensely frustrating to find that the doubt barely budged during passionate moments. This led to additional struggles. Why weren't the facts working? Could this also be a problem? Had I not studied something correctly? Here I was faced with a secondary level of uncertainty. Sometimes I just wanted to walk away from the subject altogether, but I knew that wouldn't solve my quandary.

After more years of study I concluded that although there were often factual components involved, and answers ultimately returned to the issue of whether Christianity had a solid foundation, few doubts were solved by straightforward citations of the relevant facts. This often seemed to help in the short run, sometimes substantially, but it generally lasted for only a few days. Here I am reminded of the words spoken to me years ago by a colleague: "Faith is weak when it fluctuates according to the latest archaeological discovery." Admittedly, a faith that seems to need almost daily bolstering by the facts is also in need of something else to deal with the underlying issue, something more permanent.

So the facts by themselves fail to satisfy the emotional and volitional elements of doubt. One major reason for this conclusion is that humans are whole entities—we are more than data alone. As whole persons, we need to satisfy the other components of our being, as well. Doubt is rarely a problem in the realm of facts alone. So the solution, not surprisingly, spills beyond that narrow range.

Doubt chiefly occurs to those who are intellectually gifted. It may be the case that many doubters are highly intelligent people, but that is beside the point of how it is healed. Strangely enough, this makes it more dangerous for some doubters who are used to attacking problems head-on with a good dose of "smarts." It figures that they will once again turn to what has always worked for them, but religious uncertainty usually arises for less than intellectual reasons. Unless the person goes beyond this approach for their answer, it will most likely remain impervious to correction. When you don't think your emotions are a problem, it is not surprising that you don't look there for your answers.

Once again, digging out Christianity's strong foundation is quite valuable, since it is needed at so many junctures. But we must work forward from there to other areas in order to solve many of the most common problems of uncertainty. Dealing with the issues will push one quickly enough beyond the point of the facts alone. I have tested this principle probably hundreds of times, which accounts for my practical assurance that it really works.

But we cannot overemphasize the point that the intellectual capacities of doubters is sometimes irrelevant, since many of them are not overly intellectual. This could even be a help, since this group is more likely to admit that they struggle with their emotions, thus drawing them closer to some solutions.

Doubt generally follows similar patterns. This misconception sees religious doubt as a fairly one-dimensional or single-faceted phenomenon, proceeding along uniform lines. Few things about the subject are more mistaken. Uncertainty is as varied as are the people who experience it, and comes through at least three major avenues: factual, emotional, and volitional.

Having said this, however, it is also true that, once properly identified, doubt may follow a generally similar sequence. Of course there are personal twists and turns as varied as the personal experiences of those who venture down these paths. But the adviser who understands the various facets and how they develop in each of their chief variations can often predict the trail doubt is taking in the individual. Once I determine where a person stands, I generally follow the route of attempting to predict what he or she is saying to themselves, how they feel, and so on. Usually, the person wonders how I know all this. (If they only knew the years of painful steps that led me to this point!) I think such a process often instills confidence in the doubter, because it lets them know that others have traveled this way before them. It is almost always a comfort to know that we are not alone when working through a problem area. If my prediction is inaccurate, I simply back up to the previous point, listen some more, and then try again.

All doubt can generally be solved by the same remedy or response.
This is another half-truth. If it means that there is one step that all must
apply, after which they will all get relief, then I am very skeptical. For
example, some suggest that all a person needs to do is to confess his
sins, or pray, or get more spiritual. This sounds like Job's friends, who
thought they were giving good, sound advice, yet God was not pleased
with their remedy (Job 42:7–10). To be sure, this recommendation
could work, depending on the particulars, but I think even Scripture
would suggest that solutions vary depending on the malady, and with
good reason.

If the point of the assertion is that, once a workable solution is
found, it can often be applied across the board, then this is potentially
very positive. Once again, it depends on the particulars, but in principle
it is possible. Sometimes more than one solution is very helpful.
Different and even unconventional patterns work for various people.
This is why we will provide a variety of suggestions. By analogy, physi-
cians frequently prescribe two or more medicines for the same sickness,
including varying the type or doses for different cases.

Doubt never produces positive results. We have already said many
times that religious skepticism can do harm, and can lean in the direction of unbelief or despair. But the fact that negative results *can* follow,
doesn't mean they always will. And it certainly doesn't mean that blessings cannot result. We will even take a chapter to outline some of the
positive results that can follow and have followed from the dark nights
of doubt.

We need to keep in mind that believers are not asking permission in
order to indulge in a pastime here. Most do not *want to* question their
faith; they desire fellowship with God. So, given that doubt is a reality
in their lives, its resulting in their growth and development is beneficial.

**Doubt always gets worse as one grows older, especially as one gets
closer to death.** This would seem to be a very fascinating area of

research that might yield some fruitful results. Perhaps contrary to popular conceptions, this assertion appears not to be the case. According to at least one survey (*Faith Development and Your Ministry,* Gallup, 1986) along with some other publications, older adults seem to be more settled in their beliefs and thus experience less doubt.

There are some good reasons why this is the case. Perhaps foremost on the list, developmental theory indicates that the elderly may well have moved past the formative stages of growth and come to rest in a settled sense of who they are, what life is about, and what they believe. Other considerations include the likelihood that they no longer have certain immediate worries, such as providing for their children, and there is less responsibility in general. Reasons like these could well ease the tension of questions that were more urgent earlier in life.

Once I had the privilege of interviewing an elderly Christian couple in their eighties who seemed to express a quiet, mature faith. I inquired concerning their beliefs, their worries, and their fear of death. I asked very frank questions, pushing for candid answers. As we talked, they appeared to be firm in their faith and not to be afraid to die. In fact, they strongly and confidently affirmed both. Further, they indicated that, while they had been worriers earlier in life, their present state had lasted for the previous twenty years or so. True, this is only one couple. But I sense from what I read and my own research that they are not unique in their solid, practical faith. As people mature in Christ, they are able to look back at previous experiences of God's faithfulness, with an assurance that he will be trustworthy to keep his promises in the future.

Conclusion

The falsehoods presented in this chapter were chosen because they are frequent Christian reactions to the subject of doubt. Singling them out and correcting them is crucial, but too seldom done. It is precisely because of such misconceptions that many find their own conditions so difficult to unravel. After all, if we cannot identify and locate the underlying problems, we won't know what to treat.

This leads us to one of the most important principles of this book. *To misidentify the specific nature of doubt frequently leads to looking in the wrong direction for the cure.* If I cannot determine the nature of the problem, it is certainly questionable whether I will discover the surest route to bring healing. Knowing the specific nature of the doubt allows me to see it in its clearest light and attack it from the best angle.

Just to know, for instance, that religious doubt plagues virtually everyone at some time is comforting. Realizing that it is a common human condition is heartening; it at least reveals that I am not alone in my dilemma. Further, to realize that the devastating affects of uncertainty can be cured and that the entire experience may even lead to very positive results can be equally liberating. All of this means that we need to learn more about the nature of doubt. This will be one of our upcoming goals.

We also need to be able to recognize the specific species of doubt and its general characteristics. All doubt is not created equal. It may follow various patterns and require more than one strategy before healing will take place. We have said that there are at least three distinct types (or species) of doubt. To understand the differences between each is to begin to zero in on some specific strategies with which to combat them.

Two Species
of Doubt

Secrets come in all shapes and sizes. Sometimes they are nice, and sometimes they are not. Once in a while, what they seem to be is not what they, in fact, are. But sometimes they are something special and lead to valuable discoveries. Like keys, they unlock doors to hidden treasures.

One of the best-kept secrets about religious doubt is that it comes in several forms. We have said that these variations can generally be characterized into three major species: factual, emotional, and volitional. It is crucial to understand the difference between these varieties of uncertainty. To be aware of the general characteristics and some of the root causes of each type is to get a good start in formulating a strategy for confronting it.

In this chapter, we will address the first and third types. Chapter 4 will begin our in-depth study of type two (emotional), which is the specific focus of this book. After definitions of factual and volitional doubt, we will explore a few of the underlying situations that seem to give rise to each.

Identifying Factual Doubt

Factual doubt is chiefly concerned with the foundations of religious belief and whether they are well grounded. Are there reasons for faith? Evidence for Christianity can come from many areas, for example: biblical, logical, metaphysical, historical, scientific, and even moral. The central issue concerns the warrant for religious claims, as well as giving answers to others who pose various objections.

Confronting factual doubt, then, might involve bolstering a belief by providing reasons for it. Of course, having a number of strong evidences is preferable. But strangely enough, not all reasons to believe involve producing cold, hard facts in a scientific laboratory or in a courtroom. Sometimes reasons come from seemingly unconventional arguments or sources, like the knowledge that all humans share, or the deepest longings of one's heart. Other times, counterstrikes are necessary against potential challenges to faith. This is the area of defending the Christian faith, or apologetics.

Factual doubt might come in the form of questions about the truthfulness of the Christian faith. It could pertain to biblical topics (like concerns about conflicting teachings), logical items (such as issues involving the nature of God), or other areas of philosophy (including the existence of God or the problem of evil). Still more questions could come from historical areas (like verifying the resurrection of Jesus), or scientific enterprises (such as producing evidence for design in the universe or the origin of life).

One earmark of factual doubt is that, if this is the primary type present, it should be satisfied by the various pertinent data. This assumes that such evidences and explanations are available and that they are accessible to the individual. During and since my many years of doubting, I've spent my entire professional life pursuing such avenues. I can testify that there is a staggering amount of evidence confirming theism in general, and Christianity in particular.

Of course, apologetics shouldn't be left just to professionals. The apostle Peter commanded all believers to be ready to give an answer or defense (Greek, *apologia*) for the hope that lies within them to anyone who asks (1 Pet. 3:15). This assumes that we have such answers at our disposal and that we know how to communicate them.

Karen was shocked by her college roommate's challenge that all religious belief was simply a psychological crutch.

"I have plenty of personal reasons for being a Christian," Karen responded.

"Personal reasons are not enough," her friend replied. "Unless you can point to verifiable facts confirmed by science, your belief is no more than wishful thinking."

What could she say? Since childhood, Karen had been taught that all one need do was believe through faith alone—no factual reasons were possible.

Soon after this discussion, Karen began a study of Christian evidences. In the meantime, she spoke to a Christian friend who was a philosophy major. She learned that the demand for scientific corroboration was itself not scientifically grounded. In other words, the *requirement* that one produce scientific evidence is *itself* not scientific—so it fails its own test. Here the shoe was on the other foot. Why should Karen submit to the charge to produce scientific data when her friend could give no such reason for requiring that particular demand? On what grounds should this challenge itself be feared when it had flunked its own test?

Days later, Karen's friend admitted rather sheepishly that she had no *scientific* reasons to require science as a test for truth. It had cost her some time and energy, but Karen had learned that the challenge had been an empty one. Although she didn't react like she had won a battle, Karen was greatly relieved. She may not have realized it at the time, but she was also learning two more important lessons: not all challenges are themselves properly grounded. Further, one's faith might grow stronger if one is willing to take the time to answer questions.

What seems to be a factual question, then, is sometimes argued on faulty grounds. Granted, many issues cannot be dismissed so easily. Honestly assessing challenges and providing real answers is the domain of apologetics. We will return to the topic of factual support of faith in chapter 5, although we will not be able to provide the actual evidence in this book. While facts don't always cure doubt, they are a necessary starting point—a foundation on which to build. (See the Selected Bibliography for suggested readings.)

Aggravations to Factual Doubt

Several conditions may intensify factual doubt. However, there is not a strict causal relationship between these situations and the uncertainty since we have the ability to short-circuit the process and not allow the doubt to gain a foothold. We will have more to say about this later.

Still, we will list a few problem areas that can contribute to a distressed state of mind. While there may be some overlap between the categories, each has its own distinctions. It is hoped that understanding some of the root aggravations may help us to better grasp the nature of the doubt. This is a subject where knowledge is potentially the beginning of the victory.

(1) **Factual questions.** Being asked challenging questions to one's faith is often the fastest way to experience factual doubts. After all, if we cannot be sure of the underpinnings of Christianity, how will we respond to charges? If a lack of knowledge keeps one from answering critical accusations, whatever the source, factual uncertainty is a distinct possibility.

(2) **Questioning intellect.** A source for many worries may arise from personal questions and research. While it may be a hobby that the

person really enjoys, this may backfire for any of a number of reasons: he may get too busy and have less time to spend looking for solutions, or she may outgrow the interest in perpetual curiosity, yet the questions still remain. Thus, this sort of person may gain both strength and further challenges from their intellectual pursuit.

(3) **Sidetracked by pseudoproblems.** This is another very common characteristic of this species of doubt. But unlike challenging questions and an inquisitive intellect, this one occurs when a believer is confronted by seeming problems that are not central to the truthfulness of Christianity and can deter from crucial issues. In fact, these issues don't make any substantial difference *no matter which view is taken.* In other words, whatever stand is right or wrong, faith in Christianity need not change a single iota! Questions of this nature pertain to subjects like the age of the earth, the sign gifts, eternal security, various issues in eschatology, or differing convictions concerning a Christian's separation from the world. True, these are all important questions and the Bible does say something about them. But the possible positions generally have nothing to do with the overall facticity of Christianity. Yet, these topics often get the most heated attention among believers, with combatants frequently arguing that unless their position is true, Christianity suffers in some grotesque fashion. Such is simply not the case.

This is not to say that this sort of question only surfaces among believers. Unbelievers also challenge Christians with seeming problems that don't threaten the classic truths of orthodox Christianity. Yet believers often respond as if their spiritual lives depended on the outcome.

So why do we experience this consternation? I think the chief reason, in addition to factors like pride and ignorance, is that believers far too seldom distinguish between absolutely crucial and non-crucial issues. It is often thought that everything Christians believe (whether theological, ethical, social, or political) is of equal importance. Since it is obvious that there are different expressions of orthodox Christianity (i.e., is your church Calvinistic?), these sorts of problems are bound to arise. In short, given the differences, believing that everything in Christianity is of equal weight will inevitably lead to some doubt.

Ben had been raised in the same church all of his life, and attended its Christian school. After marriage, he moved across the country and began attending a different church. It was not long before he noticed some differences. In particular, his new pastor seemed to be far more open on issues of separation from worldly pastimes, which his previous pastor had forbidden to true Christians. Being a layman and having relied all of his life on his pastor's opinions, Ben wondered if a statement that he had sometimes heard was really true after all: "The Bible depends totally on how it is interpreted. There are no objective teachings in it." Over the months, he began to struggle concerning which of his former beliefs could be trusted and which ones could not.

(4) **Worldview commitments.** Some doubts are related to struggles over issues that are only as sound as the worldview in which the position is held. In other words, rival ideas are inadequate by themselves, and can only exist as part of a larger ideology. The Christian may reject the non-Christian system but not realize that there is no problem apart from that worldview. The doubt may come from attempting to answer the challenge in a vacuum.

For example, earlier we saw that Karen was initially challenged by the contention that all religious experiences were psychological crutches. But if her friend's own worldview is mistaken, and especially if some reasons could be cited against a position that makes such charges, then the point about all personal religious experiences being subjective would seem to be questionable itself. In fact, as a well-known atheist once said to me, the knife cuts both ways here—it could be the *unbeliever* who has a psychological crutch because he does *not* wish to believe. This sort of critique gets us nowhere unless we anchor it to a system.

Knowing where doubt is coming from is half the battle. If believers know what sorts of conditions are likely to lead to factual doubt, it would make sense that they would be more prepared.

Identifying Volitional Doubt

Volitional religious doubt is chiefly concerned with one's will. It is perhaps most frequently revealed in matters such as whether an individual is willing to believe, to grow in faith, to forsake sin, or to be motivated to live the Christian life. Many times it concerns the passion with which we continue our ultimate commitment to the Lord.

At each of these points, the issue of decision making should be apparent. Volitional uncertainty, at its very heart, has to do with one's willingness to implement a choice regarding one's faith. Ironically enough, the problem might even be an unwillingness to apply certain healing techniques to the problem of doubt. In this sense, volitional aspects are present in all types of uncertainty.

Years ago Jason had several factual questions about the truthfulness of Christianity. When no one answered these to his satisfaction, he began to be affected emotionally. Following a number of unsolved bouts with his emotions, he slowly concluded that his beliefs just were not as important to him as they once had been. He was no longer motivated concerning his previous religious commitment.

Unfortunately, doubt sometimes appears to follow just such a pattern. It can progress from fairly simple (but unanswered) factual questions, through emotional quandaries, to a "deadened" plateau where the entire issue no longer appears crucial to the individual. Believers can get here through other kinds of hurts, too, like losing a loved one or being rebuffed by someone they highly esteem. But when the results affect one's will regarding one's faith, it becomes a volitional issue.

This stage is probably the most serious time of all for the person who questions, since he or she just *may not care* that they are struggling and, therefore, may not wish to do anything to stop it, including talking about what's bothering them. Unlike emotional doubt, this species may hurt the least, yet may be the most dangerous.

The key to volitional matters is to gain a new perspective on our life—to view it from God's perspective. These doubters need to get "fired up" about those things that should be of prime importance to us—that is, about God and his kingdom (Matt. 6:19–33). After all, eternal life lasts longer than our earthly existence, and promises far better quality. Further, directing our minds towards eternity improves the quality of life here on earth, as well. Jesus' message should excite the believer, since it affects both our present as well as our future. (Chapter 11 includes some suggested readings.)

Understanding volitional doubt helps us not only on its own grounds, but it provides insights into the other species of doubt, too. All doubt has a willful aspect. Let's look at some conditions that tend to irritate our resolve.

Aggravations to Volitional Doubt

As we did with factual doubt, we will state several circumstances that may contribute to and intensify volitional doubt. Again, one doesn't cause the other, but these problems can contribute to the distressed condition.

(1) **Weak Faith.** Frequently doubting believers have the sense of wishing they could increase their faith, but conclude that it is too difficult to believe any further. In James' terms, they see themselves as wavering between two positions (James 1:6–8). During my own struggles, I well remember thinking that this was a chief issue for me. How could I cause my faith to grow?

(2) **Immature faith.** Sometimes faith suffers from a lack of development, perhaps from factors stemming from the time when a person first committed her life to Christ, or from wrong ideas afterwards. Perhaps the individual was very young at the time of conversion and simply doesn't remember exactly what happened. Did I do the right thing? Was I pressured into making my decision? Was I totally committed to Christ?

While there could be emotional or other factors present, the chief issue here is one of the will: did the person truly commit herself to Christ? Whether physical immaturity was present at the time is not of prime importance. We are discussing the surrender of the will.

At this point someone may blurt out: "But that's precisely my problem. I'm not sure whether or not I initially trusted Christ and surrendered my will to him." In cases of real uncertainty as to whether a person trusted Christ, I usually encourage them to pray and express their trust in the Lord once again. They can pray the same "sinner's prayer," reciting the facts of the gospel, and tell the Lord, "If I'm already a Christian, then this is simply a prayer of further commitment. But if not, I'm trusting you right now, and bowing my will before you." This usually solves the problem of being unsure. Some may disagree with this practice, but I personally find nothing here that contradicts Scripture.

(3) **Lack of growth.** Doubt can result from the believer's failure to grow in the Christian life. Some even seem to shun the idea of getting serious with the Lord, as if getting too close to him will somehow hurt or be uncomfortable, like being sent to Africa as a missionary against one's will. Whatever the reason, not growing is a decision that can lead to uncertainty. Adding to this dilemma is that maturing in faith, in itself, is one of the chief means to stem the tide of doubt. As in human relationships, a lack of growth can lead to one drifting apart from God. Conversely, growing commitment is itself a doubt preventive.

(4) **Arrogance.** This attitude toward God creates its own brand of uncertainty. Yet it should be plain that this sort of rebellion places self above God and is not a biblical or practical breeding ground for a meaningful relationship with the heavenly Father. Unless the situation is corrected by heartfelt repentance and God's grace, it would seem that the doubt will only get worse.

(5) **Lack of repentance.** Unforgiven sin certainly contributes to a sense of separation from God, thereby encouraging doubts. The decision not to repent can be made either implicitly or explicitly, but just as this sort of situation affects the relationship between a husband and wife, it also militates against having spiritual peace.

Emily, a young woman with an outstanding Christian testimony, began experiencing some rather severe doubts about her faith after deciding that her marriage relationship was too binding. She spoke to a close friend, who didn't agree with her reasoning. Sadly, as long as Emily remained in her rebellious state, the doubts also remained. Yet, she refused to repent.

An older Christian man, Frank, was obviously depressed and hardly wanted to discuss his questions of assurance with his pastor. During their counseling, Frank admitted his years of indulging in sin and confessed that this was very possibly the reason for his spiritual uncertainty. Yet he was unwilling to change. Neither did his uncertainty diminish.

(6) **Difficulty of application.** I have saved for last one of the most common (and inexplicable) reasons why volitional doubters don't get relief. Shockingly, there is often a reluctance to apply the biblical steps for healing, even when they are known. Since it is sometimes difficult to concentrate on the application *during* the period of doubt, some conclude that it is easier to apply the steps only sporadically, or not at all. Just like pulling weeds is not fun, sometimes it is also difficult to deal with these problems in one's life. But one of the most frequent com-

ments I've ever heard is that when biblical steps are applied, the doubt diminishes or disappears. Conversely, when these steps are not taken, the uncertainty remains or returns.

This sounds similar to something we frequently hear people say regarding physical illness: When I take my medicine, I feel better. When I don't, I fail to get relief. Is it a wonder that the same principle applies to our spiritual health?

Conclusion

We have said many times that the root cause of religious uncertainty is sin. Beyond that, we are finite beings with an imperfect grasp on reality. The result is that we mess things up. Sometimes our situations get so twisted that it is exceptionally difficult to unravel them.

In this chapter we tried to identify some of the characteristics of factual and volitional doubt, along with some of the conditions that often aggravate them. These are not exhaustive lists, but hopefully they show some of the inner workings of these two species of doubt, and will contribute later to their healing.

As we have said previously, emotional uncertainty is the major focus of this book. But before we investigate it in more detail, it should be carefully noted that all species of doubt are seldom as clearly delineated as our illustrations may indicate. We are whole human beings and factual, emotional, and volitional elements overlap. Doubt is no exception; it often reveals a combination of traits.

Medical doctors are often confronted by a similar phenomenon. They must view multiple symptoms and treat the major one(s) causing the discomfort. So we must endeavor to do the same. The prominent, painful elements of doubt should be located and identified as closely as possible, so they can be treated.

Emotional Doubt:
What If . . . ?

Listen to people talk about it. Emotional pain can be the very worst hurt of all. Once I heard a person say, "I would give my right arm if I could stop doubting. No, I'm really serious. I would give it up without a second thought!" Unquestionably, emotional uncertainty can be painful. We have called it the most common and distressing of the three species of doubt. Beginning in this chapter we will turn most of our attention to this variety of questioning.

Identifying Emotional Doubt

Emotional religious uncertainty is the most common variety. It is also the most painful. Its chief cause is one's moods and passions, which explains its more subjective nature. But it regularly masquerades as factual doubt by attempting to address the same issues. Here, we will concentrate further on the nature of this frequent state of mind.

Emotional doubt is identified by the way an individual feels *about* a subject rather than judging the subject on its own merits. Of crucial importance is not the bothersome issue, whatever it is, but how the person feels about it. Distraught psychological states are sometimes evident.

The single most revealing ingredient in identifying emotional struggles is the "What if . . . ?" element. Sometimes this question is asked directly; on other occasions, it is implied. Rather than accepting the questioned data in a straightforward manner, this response is made *in spite* of the available facts, regardless of how convincing.

Allison frequently proclaimed her uncertainty about many aspects of her Christian faith. But those who listened carefully knew that she did not question the actual gospel facts of the deity, atoning death, and resurrection of Jesus Christ (which purportedly were her chief concerns). Rather, when asked why she always seemed to be in so much turmoil regarding her beliefs, Allison responded, "The gospel facts are strong, but what if Christianity just isn't true? What if, in the end, believers are simply mistaken?"

It is in this response that the true nature of Allison's doubt is identified. She did not object to the facts themselves, as some had originally thought. She was bothered by the unlikely scenario that her faith could somehow be wrong, in spite of all the evidence. It appeared that no amount of facts (even those that Allison fully accepted) could cause her to stop wondering if Christianity might be false. Here the emotional content of her doubt was revealed.

Emotional doubt frequently poses as its factual sister. It has some of the same concerns and raises some of the same questions. Yet, the issues are determined and the evidence is judged by how one feels about them. Conclusions come from one's moods or feelings. So what distinguishes emotional from factual doubt? In the former species of uncertainty, the major factor is not the actual issues that are raised, but *what is being thought and felt about them.* In typical cases, the individual's attention is not centered on the specific facts themselves, but on certain unlikely possibilities surrounding them.

Melissa was in constant turmoil as to whether she was really a Christian. She clearly remembered surrendering her life to Christ in faith, trusting him to forgive her sins. Yet, she still repeatedly wondered if she had *really* said the right words and meant them.

Bill was a believer who was regularly nagged by a fear of hell and judgment. He sometimes pictured himself standing before Jesus' throne and being told to depart to the fires of hell. This usually happened as he was trying to sleep at night. In order to deal with the pain, he started questioning whether there was, in fact, any such place as hell.

It is important to notice the main cause of Melissa's and Bill's worries. They both accepted the facts of Christianity. They both knew that there was a time when they tried, with all their heart, to trust Christ. However, their secret fear was that, for some unaccountable reason, they had unconsciously overlooked something crucial. In both cases, their doubt actually focused on the unlikely possibility that they had responded incorrectly to the Lord.

These are very typical responses for emotional doubters. This phenomenon is not so much affected by the results of careful study, as by the improbability that something has fallen between the cracks. As a result, no amount of factual evidence brings lasting peace. When a friend gave him reasons to believe in hell, Bill's fears returned with a vengeance. In fact, they grew worse.

Often the emotional doubter comes to the conclusion that their search for truth has finally ended and that all is well, only to realize a few days later that something is still amiss. This is a vicious cycle that actually wages war against the peace that periodically comes. Oddly enough, that peace is often shattered by the thought, "Why am I feeling so well today? I've still not solved problem X." Not surprisingly, the peace doesn't stay around for long.

We have said that much of emotional doubt is actually of the "What if . . . ?" variety. It may even be chiefly characterized not by what all the facts point to, but rather what minimal possibilities may still exist. Melissa and Bill suffered from just such questioning. Jason in the last chapter also went through this stage after he thought his questions were not being answered. It was almost as if they asked themselves: What's the worst possible thing that could happen to me?

The emotional doubter is often very intelligent and appears to be raising serious objections to the truthfulness of Christianity. But in reality, the uncertainty is not primarily factual and the questions are far more subjective. Human beings are able to conjure up all kinds of fears. The questions "What if Christianity is not true after all?" or "What if I am not a Christian, in spite of everything I have done?" are really no different than the "What ifs" of our society at large. "What if I get AIDS?" or "What if I flunk next week's big exam?" take the same form. Only the subject matter differs.

Who hasn't experienced these and similar worries? Why should such fears—both religious and secular—surprise us? Doesn't it make sense that we just want to be doubly sure of our most treasured values? But the problem is that this normal desire may be pushed too far, causing emotional turmoil.

It is not difficult to get emotionally distraught over the ceaseless questioning of our most cherished beliefs. This is especially so because the focus is on remote possibilities that cannot be touched by the evidence. Here is revealed one frequently forgotten aspect of this sort of doubt: it seems almost immune to the facts. A person can always counter, "Yes, I know, but WHAT IF . . . ?"

Emotional uncertainty can be a part of larger issues, too. Irritations lie at the root of these problems, often in diverse and difficult areas that span a large range, from psychological or medical problems, to child abuse, or even the death of a loved one.

Aggravations to Emotional Doubt

As we did in the last chapter with factual and volitional questioning, we need to explore several conditions that, while they don't exactly *cause* emotional doubts, do tend to escalate them. Several situations can reinforce an outlook that already has a tendency towards an anxious, worried state. Again, there may be some overlap between these categories, but each represents a unique angle. Our purpose is to provide you with information that will encourage a better grasp of this painful topic, hopefully leading to significant growth and healing.

(1) **Psychological states.** The most common irritant of emotional doubts (and perhaps even all types of uncertainty) is psychological states like anxiety or depression. It doesn't take long for agitated moods and feelings to carry over to issues regarding our faith. Our worries most frequently center on those areas that are the most meaningful to us. I have spoken to many individuals who assumed their problem had to do with evidences for faith, only to discover that their brand of questioning had to be dealt with in a different manner. The true focus had centered on their emotional state of mind, rather than the subject of evidence for faith.

(2) **Judging by feelings.** Another very common problem, especially with Christians who lack assurance of salvation, comes from reacting to situations based on one's feelings. "I don't feel the same way that I used to" or "Sometimes I don't think I'm saved" are regular fare for the counselor. The *feeling* that Christianity might not be true after all may plague all believers at some time. I am reminded of C. S. Lewis's fictional character, Uncle Screwtape, who challenged the young demon Wormwood on how to tempt Christians: "But there is a sort of attack on the emotions which can still be tried. It turns on making him *feel* . . . that all his religion has been a fantasy" (*The Screwtape Letters*, Macmillan, 1961, p. 142).

A pastor of a prominent southern church, George, called a close friend who was also a pastor and explained that his Christian walk was not as vibrant as when he first became a Christian. Although trained well at a major seminary, he had fallen into some of the same pitfalls that he had helped others through many times over the years of his ministry. After a few discussions, he realized that his questions were caused by his emotions and not by his failing faith, as he had thought. Once able to identify the area on which he most needed to work, he began to experience relief.

(3) **Medical states.** A number of medical factors can also contribute heavily to religious doubt, including internal conditions like manic depression or diabetes, as well as those caused by the consumption of alcohol or other types of drugs. To be sure, it is frequently not easy to decide which factors are most to blame. Still, while the origin of the doubt is medical, doubts that grow in this manner show up in chiefly emotional patterns.

Todd was a young graduate student who was constantly in need of counseling and tended to dominate one of the faculty member's offices. Almost on a whim, the professor noticed a certain pattern of thinking and referred him to the university clinic. Todd was diagnosed as being manic depressive and was given a prescription for appropriate medicine. After he discovered the nature of his problem, Todd also took additional steps, making tremendous strides regarding his doubt. The process took several months, but he learned that the input of the medical community was imperative to certain issues related to the treatment of doubts.

(4) **Childhood problems.** I am far from buying into Freudian principles, but it is still the case that experiences from our younger years can have a profound affect on our present doubt. For example, child abuse in various forms can make it very difficult for one to accept God's love, or to trust him.

Jill and Megan were two intelligent young women who had been abused as children, one sexually and the other physically. Megan still had a scar on her face that witnessed to this fact. Both were willing and eager to discuss their problems, but it took many sessions of discussion before each began to get control of her situation. Both women struggled with how God could ever love them when they thought that their parents never had. Their counselors found it very difficult to convince them otherwise. Jill, a student, eventually found great relief through the love of a man she later married, along with that of other family members and close friends. Megan experienced substantial healing by practicing some principles that her counselor taught her.

(5) **More recent wounds.** Painful situations throughout life can also influence religious doubt. The death of a loved one, breaking up with someone special, or betrayal by a good friend are instances of wounds that can sway a person to wonder if he can fully trust God. In this sense, the situations and results are similar to those related to childhood trauma.

(6) **Need for attention.** In some cases, the expression of doubt is due to the need for friendship and love, often from one who feels a lack in their own life. This is one of the conditions that is commonly experienced by the person who dominates the counselor's time and grows to depend on the interaction. The needy person is frequently the opposite gender of the counselor, so discernment is needed here. The doubt could certainly be real, but the need for companionship, attention, and love is perhaps even greater. If so, the problem might never get solved.

(7) **Lack of sleep and adequate diet.** A regularly overlooked aggravation of a doubting condition can sometimes be remedied simply by getting enough sleep and eating a healthy diet. A biblical example of this is Elijah, who, when he experienced depression, lay down to sleep. After he had rested, an angel recommended food (1 Kings 19:4–6).

Travis, a leader in the Christian community, came to see me with some rather troubling questions. After a little discussion we pinpointed the type of doubt he suffered as emotional and then pushed a little further for the specifics. Among other things, it became obvious that he was suffering from a lack of sleep. In fact, soon after we spoke he went to bed and woke up two days later! He decided to make an effort to get more sleep on a regular basis. Along with practicing some other principles, he began to do much better. Shortly, Travis left the area for a new ministry but kept in contact with me over many years. Every time we talked, I asked how his doubts were coming and he reported that everything was "back to normal."

(8) **Peer pressure.** I have long thought that one difficult pressure that is exerted on believers is to be more moderate in their views. This assault is not always a frontal attack (though it is increasingly becoming so), but is one that builds to quite a level in its call to trade in "old wives' tales" in favor of "modern" approaches to living. To be more like "normal" people is a desire that is difficult not to heed. Let's be honest: doesn't it hurt to think that others may think we are stupid or intolerant? If we believe that only a few intelligent people hold our position, this can produce devastating emotional results, especially over time. Often the pressure manifests in the form of a modified position on the issue in question, sometimes creating more emotional trauma. This pressure produces no new facts, just the same old temptation to change.

(9) **Imagination versus reality.** Reading fictional writings can affect us more than we might think. Even more influential are graphic movie and television dramatizations that bring us face to face with people and ideas. Here we meet a subtle temptation to identify with the problems of the characters and view issues of good and evil through *their* eyes, instead of through our own worldview.

Years ago I watched a popular science fiction movie. I was so caught up with the plot that I found myself despairing because of the evil in the world. I am embarrassed to say that for about half an hour my own perception was colored until I realized the obvious: I was witnessing someone else's unreal conception of the issues! But if such subtleties are allowed to go unchecked, one could experience emotional doubts simply by identifying with others.

(10) **Christian hypocrisy**. Doubt sometimes skyrockets after observing the beliefs and actions of fellow Christians. Unjust wars, tortures, persecutions, and other crimes have all unquestionably been carried out in the name of Jesus Christ. And this is not to mention secret sins that periodically have been made public and splashed across media headlines. How sad is the effect on the lay person when their pastor or another spiritual leader falls! While these are horrors that certainly need to be addressed, they do not touch the truthfulness of the Christian worldview at all. Christianity is not affected by what others have done in its name. These are two differing trails that do not intersect.

On the other hand, confronting our own failures, as a reminder of the sin from which God has rescued us, as well as providing impetus for further action against it, can be healthy, if kept in perspective.

(11) **Unforgiven sin**. The fear that one's sins have never really been forgiven has always been a prominent reason for many believers to doubt. Making matters worse is the idea that one has committed the unpardonable sin so that one *cannot* be forgiven, striking even more fear in some believers' hearts. Could anything be worse to the sensitive Christian?

Fred shocked his adult Sunday school class one day by expressing a horrifying fear. He believed the very fact that he had asked questions about God from time to time, sometimes passionately, might mean that he had committed the unpardonable sin. The class leader pointed out Fred's implied but highly emotional "What if . . . ," and reminded the class that we could raise this scary question in any situation. Wisely, the leader remarked that this popular conception about doubt was mistaken. Many well-known Bible characters had challenged God and are today known as heroes of the faith. Doubt needed to be dealt with, and could lead to negative results, so Fred should not take it lightly. But this was not the same as having committed the unpardonable sin.

(12) **Anxiety about the future.** It is not enough that many Christians worry about the present; anxiety concerning the unknown future also causes a degree of fear in most believers at some time or another. For some, it might be the uncertainty that their faith can really "hold out" until the end, perhaps in the context of persecution. But God never asks us to hold out by the sheer force of our wills. A study of Scripture is certainly needed, but this alone will probably not solve the problem once our emotions become involved. At some point, the latter obstacle needs to be addressed as well.

(13) **Faulty view of God.** To have a wrong concept of God can be a seed that germinates into a full-blown case of emotional doubt. While no believer has a perfect view of God, some errors are more harmful than others. For instance, to believe that God does not answer prayers, especially during times of stress, or that he is morally responsible for pain, can lead to a personal crisis. To say that bad theology can have this kind of influence on our walk with God will surprise some believers, but it is a subject that deserves our constant inspection and correction.

(14) **Judgment and hell.** Even among believers there are some who encounter the fear that perhaps it is possible to have done everything that the Bible requires for salvation (as far as one knows) but still be sent to hell. Needless to say, this makes the prospect of judgment a rather "iffy" situation!

Over the years, I have asked dozens of adult groups this question: "How many of you, after salvation, have ever considered the possibility of being sent to hell?" If these informal surveys can be trusted, this fear is very widely experienced by many Christians at some time or another. Here we find another misbelief: that Jesus Christ may send true believers to hell. Yet the Bible provides many assurances of salvation, and we need to forcefully confront and contradict this thought whenever it enters our minds.

As this brief list indicates, there are probably more potential aggravations to emotional doubt than to any other species. This should not be surprising, since it is so common and comes in so many forms. Obviously, there is a crucial need to deal with this type of uncertainty.

Conclusion

Here we have a good news-bad news scenario. The negative side involves the very nature of emotional doubt—that many believers are affected, and it can be very painful when it enters our lives. The good news is that gaining relief from the pain of emotional doubt is often easier than we might think. The majority of cases can be substantially relieved with less effort than it takes to combat other sorts of problems. But it may have to be treated regularly and systematically. There are a number of specific strategies for healing that can be employed, even if you, like me, are neither a medical doctor, psychologist, nor professional counselor. We will spend the rest of this volume dealing with various aspects of this subject.

5

A Solid Foundation

Years ago I spoke at Stanford University on the subject of religious doubt. I addressed most of my comments that afternoon to the topic of emotional questions about faith. During the discussion afterwards, a student offered an especially penetrating protest that I have repeated in many of my lectures since. He said, "Of course these techniques you are suggesting will work—they are based on sound psychological principles. But this amounts to nothing more than mind bending. We may change our *perspective* on the subject, yet that's all that really changes."

This student was objecting that, while we may alter our thinking in order to avoid the accompanying pain in our lives, it was all simply a cerebral exercise. True, we may thereby eliminate the mental anguish, but what additional benefit was there in the "real world"? I had to admit that it was an impressive complaint, indeed.

I responded, "Your charge is totally correct—*if* Christianity is not true. *If* the Christian faith is not true to reality, then, yes, all we can hope for is the quieting of the emotional pain in our lives. Let's just note in passing that this would still be a very positive effect in itself. Yet, as helpful as that might be, we would—as you put it—only be mind bending. But," I continued, "the entire issue rests on whether Christianity is true. If so, it then becomes a more direct issue of whether we will *apply* that truth to our thinking. In other words, if reality *is* shaped along the lines of the Christian faith, then we have a twofold truth here. We have the truth of the message itself, and then we are left with the challenge of whether we will apply it to our lives. Will we personally fill the prescription and employ the remedy? If we *fail* to apply it, we are *not* living in accord with the real world! The tables have completely turned on us!"

The student did not offer a follow-up response.

This is nothing short of an astounding realization for many of us. If Christianity is not true, all we can hope for by applying our approach is to still the emotional pain. This would seem a noteworthy goal in itself, since this is what caused the person to seek help in the first place. After all, when we go to a physician, we want healing, not the answer to all of our philosophical questions!

On the other hand, if Christianity is true, we have two trophies for the price of one. Not only do we have a salve for our emotional pains, but we also have the proper background that guarantees a more lasting, eternal balm. Like having medicine for our deepest emotional hurts in the present; and eternal reality for the future, all at our fingertips! What more could we possibly ask for?

But remember, we have to *choose* both to believe the truth and apply the emotional ointment. If we decide to forego either one, we receive much less benefit than we otherwise would.

Years ago, I began to discover this wonderful truth in my life during my own times of doubt. But it didn't come without intense struggle, and when it did come, it was in a disguised form. I was surprised—and a little angry—that knowing the facts alone didn't totally heal the hurt, although at least they usually kept the infection from spreading! Back I would go to my studies.

The point here is that, unless a solid basis exists, any effort to solve doubts might be viewed as a mind game. Admittedly, it may still be the aspirin we need for the pain of the moment, but as the student had pointed out, we want something that is true in the "real world," too. We want more than temporary relief. If Christianity is true, then strategies that are based on this foundation are well grounded.

So that We might Know

So is Christianity true? Do we have the basis that we need in order to build the best possible foundation for the remainder of this book?

This is not an apologetics textbook. Evangelicalism is privileged, however, to have literally *dozens* of such volumes at its fingertips. At least an introductory treatment of many of these items will be provided by the sources listed in chapter 11, "Selected Bibliography." Topic divisions along with a brief annotation of each volume may provide some tips concerning where one might look for specific answers.

Theism

In this chapter, we will have to be content with the briefest of overviews of some of the avenues at our disposal. Christianity *does* have a solid, factual foundation that exists on two levels. It can be shown, first of all, that theism is true. This means that a personal God exists who is the Creator of the universe, but who remains separate from the creation. This being has a relation to the limited, changing persons who live in the world he created. At this first level we cannot differentiate between theistic religions, but we can learn several crucial truths. Naturalism, which teaches there is no supernatural realm whatsoever, is the "odd man out" if theism is true. Pantheism, with its frequent emphasis on an impersonal force, also loses if theism is true. Interestingly, Scripture makes some of these same claims.

That a theistic God exists is evident from the existence of the world (Heb. 3:4). Anything that is finite, beginning to exist at a point in time, needs a cause. Contemporary astrophysics clearly teaches that the universe came into being about 15 billion or so years ago. Regardless of how old the universe actually is, if it began to exist at a certain time, then it is finite. As such, it needs a cause for its existence.

The presence of life in the universe also needs an adequate explanation (Acts 17:28). Even a lowly amoeba depends for its existence on the presence of DNA, the building block of life. Yet the DNA of the amoeba, which makes the organism what it is, contains more information than exists in many scholarly libraries of books! Since DNA is absolutely required in order for life as we know it to exist, all DNA could not have evolved after the first of earth's organisms. We're not talking here about a spark of light or bolt of lightning somehow mysteriously causing the first one-celled creature in a primeval sea, with the DNA coming along later. We must explain the DNA as a fact that guides the beginning of life. This needs to be adequately explained. But how can this incredibly complex strand of information originate by chance? How could this burst of information co-exist with the initial, one-celled life? Does this appear, at face value, to be the work of a haphazard universe, or one that is orderly and headed in a specific direction (cf. Ps. 19:1–4; Rom. 1:19–20)?

There are many other building blocks of life, too. A single enzyme requires the lineup of a number of amino acids. These amino acids must come in a specific order, without exception. To use the Arabic alphabet as an example, an enzyme requiring fifteen amino acids would have to have a line up in A-B-C . . . M-N-O order. If even a single amino acid was out of line or in another order, the enzyme would not result. And yet, there are some who would have us believe that the existence of every single enzyme is due to random ordering that just happened to be right, rather than what it more clearly points toward—the work of a Creator who had a specific plan for creation.

Morality is not just a list of dos and don'ts that someone invented to make us miserable, or to keep order in our society. There is an intrinsic right and wrong in the universe that, if ignored, leads to physical and spiritual chaos (Rom. 2:14–15). The presence of morality is an indicator not only that God created the physical components of the universe, but the relational ones as well, and that our lives and relationships are healthiest when we "follow the rules."

Evidences for life after death are also strong indicators pointing toward a personal God. For example, near-death experiences that are independently verifiable suggest that some component of our being survives the death of the physical body. Like morality, this presents a major roadblock for naturalism.

All of these characteristics of the world in which we live—the finite universe, the prerequisites for lifelike DNA and enzymes, signs of objective morality, and verifiable accounts of consciousness after death—argue that we are not accidents in an impersonal universe. The truthfulness of theism is a far better explanation for all these facts than the theory that it all evolved independently of design.

Christianity

The second level of response is that Christianity is the specific form of theism that best accounts for other data. This can be seen from several more levels of evidence, each of which is both more specific and more personal than the general indicators for theism that we just mentioned. As with theism, Scripture also uses arguments like these in order to show the truth of Christianity.

Fulfilled prophecy argues powerfully that there is a God, and he is intricately involved in the march of human history. God even proposes prophecy as a test that he is Lord (Isa. 41:21–24; 45:20–22). Three areas that need to be investigated are those of distinctive city and nation predictions, specifications concerning Israel, and details pertaining to the coming of God's chosen Messiah. I think the best overall case is one that is constructed of a few quality predictions in each category, the examples being those that were plainly predicted beforehand and clearly pertain only to the events in question, in order to rule out vagueness and manipulation. In such instances, the more specific these prophetic details are, the stronger the predictive value that results.

Jesus' miracles are seldom used today in Christian apologetics, but are still a worthwhile evidence in an overall case for Christian theism. Jesus claimed several times that his miracles indicated that his message was true (for examples, Mark 2:10–12; Luke 7:20–22). His followers agreed (John 20:30–31; Acts 2:22). These events are exceptionally well attested, being found in every level of the four Gospels, and are even affirmed by Jesus' enemies. Several miracles are attended by intriguing historical details that can be independently verified, or offer other marks of authenticity. Recent examples from current medical literature, for example, reveal some fascinating parallels that can argue that God is similarly active today. For reasons like these, contemporary critics treat these aspects of the Gospel narratives very seriously.

Without question, the chief verification of Christian theism comes from the resurrection of Jesus. This extraordinary event can be shown to be historical even when only a bare minimum of historical facts is used, each of which is admitted by unbelieving critical scholars today, as well as being strongly attested by the known data. Further, alternative attempts to dismiss the resurrection on natural grounds have failed to account for the same data, as even these same critics generally admit. In the New Testament, both Jesus (Matt. 12:39–40; 16:4) and his apostles (Acts 2:22–24; 17:31) pointed to the resurrection as the chief sign that he was God's messenger.

That the Bible is a trustworthy document can be shown through a variety of avenues: manuscript number, copying accuracy, archeology, geography, extrabiblical confirmation, ancient legal and other customs, as well as other studies concerning the dates and authorship of the writers of the individual books. The inspiration of Scripture is also a crucial truth, confirmed by evidences like by fulfilled prophecy which no human could have orchestrated on his own (cf. Deut. 18:17–22). Jesus' miracles are helpful in this regard, too (John. 14:11). The strongest argument for inspiration is that this was the testimony of Jesus, whose teachings were confirmed by his resurrection from the dead.

A crucial component of Christianity concerns the deity of Jesus Christ. Not only are Jesus' claims concerning himself (especially as indicated by the titles "Son of Man" and "Son of God") established on very strong textual grounds; they are vindicated by the prophecies he fulfilled, the miracles he performed, the life he lived, and especially by his own resurrection from the dead. The latter was the chief indication that God confirmed Jesus' teachings (Acts 2:22–24; 17:31), and his deity, in particular (Rom. 1:3–4). After all, God would not raise a heretic from the dead.

Additionally, there are extremely potent answers to the objections that are raised by critics of Christianity. Each challenge has been thoroughly researched and explained by competent scholars, the result being a large body of data arguing that Christianity is both self-consistent and true. Further, believers have found that their beliefs make sense out of life like no other system does, making life worthwhile.

In summary, a wide range of fulfilled prophecies, Jesus' miracles, his resurrection from the dead, the nature and origin of Scripture, and the deity of Jesus Christ are all formidable arguments for the truthfulness of Christianity. Each plays a key role in showing that this is the proper approach to God.

While witnessing, Richard was asked a question that he couldn't answer adequately. Even though he sensed that he fumbled with the answer, the person to whom he was speaking seemed to be satisfied. Still, Richard grew more bothered about the subject. So he visited with a friend who was well read in the area of apologetics. Amazingly, Richard's question was answered thoroughly in just a matter of minutes.

"Thanks so much," Richard called out lightheartedly as he waved and left his friend's house. His satisfaction on the issue, even in the days ahead, showed that his doubt was factual in nature.

Other World Religions

In an age where the earth seems to have grown smaller and world religions have broken beyond their traditional boundaries, rival religious claims are more common every day. Many Americans know non-Christians personally, such as the Hindus living in our neighborhoods or the Muslims who work with us side by side. Without question, these situations have compounded Christian doubt. How can Christianity still be considered to be unique, as it teaches?

Just as we live in strange times, the answer to this question is also strange. Surprisingly, Jesus had no real challengers among the founders of the major religious groups. None of them claimed to be God, let alone taught that they were a unique, one-of-a-kind, divine manifestation of the almighty. Buddha was very possibly an atheist! Confucius and Lao Tzu were teachers of ethics, not theologians. Abraham, Moses, and David never came close to teaching that they were deity. Neither did Mohammed, who is believed by the Muslim faithful to be Allah's chief prophet but who under no condition considered himself to be deity.

Neither do the orthodox followers of the other major world religions believe that their founders rose from the dead. There is no credible evidence that anything like this ever happened in any case other than that of Jesus Christ. In fact, there is very little that might even be called historical evidences in these belief systems. All of this is certainly significant.

At the college that Aimee attended, she often heard that other religions made very similar claims to those made by her Christian friends. It made sense to her that this was the case—wouldn't believers in other faiths view their founders similarly to her perspective of Jesus? She assumed that this applied to her Buddhist roommate, too, but this conclusion led to questions whenever her pastor preached that Christianity was unique. She decided to do a study in this area for an upcoming research paper.

Aimee was both relieved and amazed to discover that Buddhists do not claim that Buddha was God. Her roommate didn't even know whether or not she was a theist. Further, claims that Buddha performed miracles were taken from religious texts that dated literally hundreds of years after the wise man died. Lastly, Aimee discovered no contentions that he was ever raised from the dead. When questioned, her friend simply shrugged off the disparity of evidence that Buddhism was true.

"I guess there are some major differences, then, and in some critical areas, too," Aimee concluded. Thereafter, she was very careful not to sound haughty when talking to her friend. Yet she was very pleased with the results of her research.

Seeking and Finding God

Our brief look at some of the factual arguments for Christianity is only one side of the coin, however. Judging from the literature, we might get the impression that many Christians don't really care that there is so much evidence for their faith. It is often said that the present generation is seeking to "experience" God rather than "know" him intellectually. Far from wanting more factual ammunition in their search for truth, they might ask how they can encounter God more fully.

This question is also relevant to doubt. The issue of whether God interacts with us today haunts many, even as it did in biblical times. Is he active in our lives? Why doesn't he reach out to us in tangible ways more than he does? If personal experience is as important as we are led to believe, then this is a legitimate concern.

Some scholars think that God respects our freedom enough that he doesn't force himself on us. He is content to lure us to himself by various means, sharing some brief glimpses of what more fellowship with him would be like, without obliging us to seek him. Those who wish to turn from their sin and believe may do so (Rom. 6:20–23) by the power of the Holy Spirit, while those who, for whatever reason, are content not to do so will separate themselves from God, as they appear to desire (Rom. 1:18–32).

Why would this be God's approach? Is it that he desires our love and fellowship without coercion? As the old saying goes, God may have decided that it was better to have loved everyone and lost some than never to have loved any of us at all. Therefore, he wants those who come to him to do so because of their own choice. This is how much he respects the free will with which he created us.

There might be an analogy here to finding a spouse. If we had the ability to force someone to love us merely by making a mental decision, we might momentarily entertain the possibility of activating that choice. Yet I think that, as enticing as it might appear, most of us would concede that such forced love is ultimately not worth pursuing. There is hardly any question that love that is freely given is better by far. Judging by how he created us, it seems that God apparently thinks so, too.

On this thesis, it seems apparent that enough evidence exists to convince those who look for God with an open mind, yet not enough to absolutely prove the truth to those who prefer to ignore him. Those who respond to the wooing of the Holy Spirit find God (Acts 17:1–4; 1 Cor. 2:11–15; 2 Cor. 5:16–21), while those who freely reject him get their wish, too.

So where do we go from here? Since God has provided more than enough evidence for those who are open to it, the question is not why there isn't more data. The real question is whether we will choose to believe and follow him. Like little children who tire of one toy after another on Christmas day, we throw aside God's gifts, demanding that he give us more. But there are already far more than enough presents to make us eternally happy. We just need to slow down and see what he has *already done*.

One way to follow God and cultivate a relationship with him is to practice regularly the so-called spiritual disciplines: Bible meditation, personal worship, fasting, simplicity, service, getting alone with God for times of silence, and so on. The main idea here is that Scripture teaches a variety of ways for the believer to know God on a deeper, more intimate level. While reading the Bible, witnessing, Christian fellowship, and some level of prayer are popular among believers, we frequently avoid those disciplines which require more time and effort. This is a very large subject and many recent books have been written on the topic. We will make some reading suggestions in chapter 11.

Conclusion

What does all of this have to do with the subject of doubt? It is precisely *because* Christianity has such a firm foundation that strategies dealing with religious uncertainty are so well established. Not only is the Christian faith true, bringing eternal life to those who trust in God's path, but it is also practical—it still changes lives today and points the way to a meaningful, lasting relationship with God. Like the answer to the Stanford University student mentioned previously in this chapter, since Christianity is true, we are making the wrong move if we don't take the proper steps of application.

Yet, while having a firm foundation that is grounded in the facts can help deal with problems pertaining to the truth of Christianity, it seldom calms the more raging sorts of worries that come from our emotions or volition. However, it still provides the basis that is necessary in order to move on to these other areas. It is crucial that there be such a backdrop of truth. In the next chapter we will explain that the primary answer to emotional doubt is not to provide more evidence. Rather it is to deal with our feelings toward the evidence and how they impact our personal lives.

Mapping a Specific Strategy

Emotional dilemmas occur to all of us. No matter who we are, everyone gets bothered from time to time, some of us more frequently and easily than others. But it is especially convicting when you have written and lectured so frequently on similar topics!

Once I was fretting about something that was so serious that I no longer even remember the subject, though I've tried. (Isn't that typical?) My wife, who had often heard me lecture on emotional doubt, walked through the room while I fumed about the long-forgotten scenario. As she passed me, rolling her eyes in mock frustration, I heard her say, "What if. . . ? What if . . . ? What if . . . ?" Her voice trailed off as she passed around the corner and out of sight.

How convicting! I had been caught! I can assure you that I stopped my worrying on the spot.

Precisely because Christianity has a solid foundation (as we have just discovered in the previous chapter), we can now launch out into well-grounded strategies that address the problem of emotional doubt. In dealing with such feeling-oriented problems, we must progress beyond the facts themselves to the truth that comes from them. Before we begin, however, we need to be very clear that the methodology we will favor in this chapter is not the only way to deal with emotional uncertainty. Neither is our specific list of steps the only approach to healing. Combining strategies can be very helpful. To that end, we will explore some other options in the next two chapters.

Here we will concentrate chiefly on those doubts that seem to come from anxious worry, as opposed to other emotional struggles. This focus is deserving because these doubts may well be the most common variety, as well as potentially the most painful. They cry out for a remedy.

One last note should be mentioned before we begin. The biblical approach we are about to investigate is not a "self-help" scenario. We do not act by the sheer force of our willpower. The power to change a Christian's emotional doubt comes from the Lord (cf. Zech. 4:6); and the weapons are his (2 Cor. 10:3–4). Our personal efforts and the application of certain techniques are commanded, but these are not the source of the healing.

A Strategy for Healing Emotional Doubt

How do we begin the process of conquering emotional doubt? We will stretch the process out over three chapters in order to give you plenty of ammunition from which to pick and choose a remedy that best meets your needs. In this chapter, we will look briefly at a crucial Bible passage that deals with worry. Then we will present some further strategies to help implement this biblical advice.

A Biblical Pattern

The Bible contains various kinds of instruction for those who suffer distress. Therefore, we are careful not to offer advice from a single passage as if to say it's the only avenue for relieving a hurtful situation. At the same time, one text, in particular, is very helpful in dealing with anxiety.

The apostle Paul addressed the subject of anxious worry in Philippians 4:6–9. Although doubt is not his chief target, questioning that comes from an anxious spirit can still be treated in this way. Rather than exegeting the text, we want to draw some specific conclusions concerning religious doubt. This is a very profound passage that promises God's peace to those who apply the principles to life.

After telling the Philippian believers to rejoice (v. 4), Paul addresses the issue of anxiety. His language indicates that these Christians were *currently* in a state of worry *(meden merimnate)*, which is an encouragement to us when we suffer from similar symptoms of anxiety or doubt. Paul's advice here is to pray and petition God with our requests (4:6). While Paul doesn't give us many details about what this means (cf. 1 Thess. 5:16–18), Peter provides some advice on the same subject in 1 Peter 5:7. The apostle tells us to give our anxieties to the Lord and to leave them with him, which is probably what Paul meant by petitioning God with all prayer and supplication. These burdens are not for us to carry. So this is our starting point.

During my time of doubt, I once heard a speaker ask, "Why worry when you can pray?" I distinctly remember my caustic response: "The only person this advice will help is the one who isn't worrying in the first place! The minute you give something to the Lord, it comes right back!"

But we ought not stop here, since Paul makes some further suggestions. After the initial step, he encourages the believer to make thanksgiving a vital part of the prayer! (v. 6). Later he mentions praising God (v. 8b). While thanksgiving and praise are not the same, I think they combine to make a powerful, but too seldom practiced, technique for the treatment of doubt.

Philippians 4:7 reveals God's promised results: peace that passes human understanding, which guards or "keeps" our minds in Christ Jesus. The word sometimes translated "keep"*(phroureo)* is a military term indicating to "guard" or to "garrison." God's peace acts as a fortress that protects the believer's mind.

In order to test this hypothesis, I very frequently ask a question of my audience when I lecture on this subject. "How many of you have ever, either intentionally or unintentionally, spent at least ten minutes thanking God for a blessing and/or praising him precisely *during* a time of doubt?" Without fail, hands shoot up across the room. "What happens when you respond to your situation in this manner?" Without rehearsing or hinting at the reply I am seeking, and *without exception,* someone calls out: "Whenever I do this, my mood changes. My doubt subsides." Although this is admittedly an informal survey, many believers have testified that Paul's advice about thanksgiving and praise is worth its weight in gold. It is difficult to experience anxiety during concentrated efforts to honor and worship God.

Besides praying and thanksgiving, Paul goes on to explain that believers need to occupy their minds with godly thoughts (4:8). They ought to concentrate on those things that are true *(alethes),* honorable or holy *(semnos),* righteous *(dikaios),* clean or pure *(hagnos),* on that which provokes love *(prosphiles),* or whatever has a good reputation *(euphema).* Two other possible categories for concentration are those thoughts that are excellent in virtue or moral quality *(arete)* and whatever deserves praise *(epainos).* The Christian ought to focus on truths such as these. Paul's last verb, "to think" *(logizomai),* indicates a stronger action than simply casual attention. It refers to the process of *habitually dwelling* or reflecting on a topic. This is the biblical practice of meditation—filling our minds deeply and single-mindedly with God's truth.

Jeremy was a student who regularly questioned his faith: could Christianity *just possibly* be false? This uncertainty gnawed at him continually, in spite of there being no evidence to support his fear. He did not resolve this dilemma until he first learned to constantly remind himself that *anything* could be questioned by such feelings—his finances, his health, even his exam next week. Then he began confirming within himself the truth, based on Scripture, that he *was* a believer. Faithfully he rehearsed this fact every time he began to worry, until he achieved substantial relief.

Finally, the single-minded meditation on proper thoughts that Paul calls for needs to be practiced *(prasso)* until it becomes a habit (4:9). Christian "modeling" is also evident in this verse, as Paul, the mature believer, serves as a guide for other Christians.

This passage provides at least four biblical steps for treating anxiety like that which might accompany emotional doubt. These steps may be listed as follows:

(1) prayer of petition

(2) thanksgiving and praise

(3) edifying thinking

(4) practice and Christian modeling.

In the last chapter we mentioned the exercise of the classic Christian disciplines as a means of increasing our fellowship with God. It should be noted that each of these steps denotes separate regimens for the believer to develop and practice. Alone they represent powerful means of seeking God, but together, they are nothing short of an awesome array of four weapons that we are to employ during our emotional struggles.

In short, the problem should be committed to God in prayer, with thanksgiving and praise, with believers exchanging their old, anxious thoughts for God's truth. This ought to be practiced until it becomes a habit, or a way of life. Paul attests that the application of these truths promotes healing and peace to those who follow the prescription. His overall teaching is that Christians need to stop worrying, by changing their anxious thoughts, including doubts, for wholesome ones.

Exchanging our Anxious Thoughts for God's Truth

I am not a psychologist. I realize that many believers are suspicious that the theories and techniques used by psychologists are not always based on Scripture, and sometimes with good reason. Yet, I don't think this justifies "throwing the baby out with the bathwater," as the saying goes. After years of personal research on many related subjects, I think the better approach is to make use of those psychological techniques that are true to Scripture. Some teachings by Christian psychologists frankly do not conform to God's Word, while other counselors utilize excellent techniques that make the most of exceptionally helpful insights gleaned from Scripture. Since any truth ultimately goes back to the Creator, we should not avoid it when it meets the scriptural standard.

I have come to the conclusion that certain forms of the "cognitive method" are the closest to Scripture, with specific behavioral techniques providing follow-up application. The cognitive method is based on the principle that change begins in our thinking, working out into our emotions and will. Therefore, clear, biblical thinking must be applied to our whole lives: to how we feel, to the things we tell ourselves, and what we decide to do. In this book, we are chiefly interested in applying biblical truth and thinking to our painful emotions.

How could believers object to this? Doesn't this sound like Paul's advice in Philippians 4:8? We have seen that the apostle exhorts believers to exchange their worrisome thoughts for God's truth, emphasizing edifying thinking patterns rather than the faulty ones that lead to the anxiety that he describes in verse 6. We must meditate on God's instructions instead of our own emotions.

But this can be a very difficult assignment, especially in the middle of our anxieties. I have seen many doubters who understand the principles, but who just do not seem to be able to apply them when they are most needed. Is this really surprising? We've already said that Paul's readers were also currently in a state of anxiety. That's why he wrote these things to them. It's not that these techniques fail to work. In fact, believers just seem at times to be impotent to make the application, even though they readily admit that when they apply the instructions, they *do* work. Paul commands that we change our thinking. Some additional pointers on how to apply his teaching might be helpful here.

Many recent books have encouraged believers to think differently, in keeping with God's truth. Chapter 11 contains an annotated list of some of these volumes. Two Christian psychologists who support such an effort are William Backus and Marie Chapian. One of their co-authored volumes, (*Telling Yourself the Truth* [Minneapolis: Bethany House, 1980]), is not specifically addressed to the issue of religious doubt but presents sound techniques for dealing with emotional struggles of all different sorts. Their particular method, termed "misbelief therapy," is applicable to emotional doubts. In this section, I will present some of their ideas, making specific application to those who question their faith. Page numbers in parentheses can be traced to the above book.

Backus and Chapian explain that our feelings are largely caused by what we say to ourselves. So if we tell ourselves untruths or lies, those thoughts can certainly cause us harm. These misbeliefs "are the direct cause of emotional turmoil, maladaptive behavior and most so-called 'mental illness'" (p. 17). Even those things that we fear most, like embarrassments or failures, do not usually cause us as much emotional havoc as do our misbeliefs *about* them. *"What you think and believe determines how you feel and what you do"* (p. 22, emphasis theirs).

For example, if a Christian repeatedly tells him or herself that Christianity may not be true, or that they may be going to hell, it should not be surprising that they begin to believe it after awhile. At this point, what the Christian is saying is contrary to his deepest desires.

Thus, conflict is sure to be the result unless there is a change in these unbiblical thoughts. Later, improper behavior may also reflect these untrue thoughts.

Backus and Chapian assert that the correct response to these misbeliefs is a threefold strategy that is reminiscent of the last two steps of our biblical pattern from Paul. Their approach is outlined in the following steps (p. 15, emphasis theirs):

1. *Locate your misbeliefs.*
2. *Remove them.*
3. *Replace misbeliefs with the truth.*

We need to *listen* to ourselves in order to *pick out* the lies that we say to ourselves every day. These misbeliefs then need to be *removed,* which is done by arguing against them. Here we need to respond to ourselves forcefully: "No, that is not true, because. . . ." Lastly, God's truth is supplied in place of the lies. We do not simply dismiss the anxious thoughts, but *replace* them with truths like those Paul mentions in Philippians 4:8. We think godly thoughts instead of the anxious ones.

Backus and Chapian challenge the hurting person to control their own emotions. God has even commanded us to do so. The real issue, then, is whether or not we will follow God's prescription:

> ". . . you *can* change your emotions . . . no matter
> what you have experienced in your life and no matter
> what your circumstances are" (p. 24, emphasis theirs).

The first time Tracey heard that she could control her emotions and thus bring relief to her anxiety, she objected: "Maybe others can be healed like that, but it won't work with me. I've already tried everything, but nothing works." The battle was over for her before it even started—*she had made a choice* not to use her prerogative to choose! In other words, she didn't believe that she could control her thoughts by simply choosing to do so; thus her choice to do nothing ruled out the possibility of healing.

Hold it right there! What is the nature of Tracey's complaints? Essentially, she was telling God that the prescriptions in his Word against worry don't really work, after all! Her comments need to be directly identified for what they are: misguided thinking.

Whenever we catch ourselves thinking that our misbeliefs are true, we must stop ourselves *immediately* and correct the thoughts. How is that done? By working through each of Paul's four steps in Philippians 4:6–9, then applying the three rules suggested by Backus and Chapian as one way of implementing Paul's command in verse 8 to change our thinking. It is possible to get so used to this sequence that we can quickly identify the misguided thoughts on the spot and perform the entire exercise in a short amount of time. As we get better at it, we progress to the point where we seldom think the lies in the first place. That is, indeed, a happy realization: victory!

So now we see where the blame for the faulty thinking is to be placed: squarely on the shoulders of the one who is suffering. There are few more profound truths on this subject: *people and events around us can't force us to doubt or worry.* We can't blame our emotions on them. The key is *how we respond* and how we interpret the occurrences in our lives. Changing our wrong beliefs really does alter both our feelings and our actions. While our outward circumstances may not change immediately, what we *tell ourselves* about them *can* change right away, and this is where the problem is. The change in ourselves may be gradual, but it *can* happen; our problems *can* be remedied (pp. 14, 17, 24–27).

How does all of this apply to emotional doubts? The first time I ever heard this last assertion, I missed the point completely. "So what if what I tell myself changes immediately?" I asked myself often. "The problems that are causing my grief have not yet gone away."

This thinking just proved that I had not yet internalized God's truth. External problems *do not and cannot* force me to doubt. The doubt doesn't come until I give myself permission to question. The uncertainty, then, is *caused by my own, private thought life;* and by allowing myself to continue to be anxious, I am clearly disobeying Paul's commands. *If what I am telling myself can change immediately, then I am already on my way to healing my doubt with the truth.* What a bombshell!

For example, instead of thinking that believers may be sent to hell or that Christ may someday abandon us, Christians need to object, and replace these lies with the truth: "Jesus does *not* send saved people to hell. I know this to be true based on the authority of the resurrected Christ himself. The Lord of the universe loves me and I have a unique place with him" (John 3:16–18; Rom. 8:28–39; Eph. 1:3–14). Or, instead of Jeremy's earlier concern whether Christianity could be false, he learned to stop questioning immediately and point out the misbeliefs. He could doubt anything on the grounds of mere possibility alone, but it is unwise to base our lives on this kind of thinking. A review of Christian evidences helped, too. Jeremy learned that he needed to strengthen his faith by daily practice, rather than by allowing emotional questions to trample him underfoot.

Shannon often experienced times when her moods were troublesome. Particularly during these moments she was prone to "feel" unsaved. "It's like denying what is most important in my life," she frequently told her closest friends. "This is incredibly painful." Then one of her pastor's sermons helped her to see what she was doing, and she began to react to her moods by directly confronting them. "Feelings are irrelevant to my salvation," she forcefully declared. Then she reinforced this truth with some appropriate biblical texts that she wrote down and kept with her at all times. She even memorized verses that described her true condition and blessings in Christ. The more practiced she became at reciting these truths, the better she felt. That was all the encouragement she needed to continue preaching to herself.

When we do not "feel" saved we must not allow a frequent course of events to take place: an emotional letdown and further "What iffing," followed later by a "Who cares?" attitude. Like a cold splash of water in the face, we could jolt ourselves with the question, *"Who cares how I feel?"*

Whenever we do not "feel" saved, we need to ask ourselves a pointed question: since when do our feelings determine whether or not we are saved? As Shannon learned, reinforcements can come from follow-up truth statements composed of relevant biblical texts.

Dana wondered why God did not answer prayer today, as he clearly did in biblical times. After months of frustration, he finally decided to seek the counsel of a friend, who challenged him to share in a Bible study. Later, Dana declared his surprise discoveries to his Sunday school class: "We found that many Bible heroes asked this very same question, seemingly without answers. Job, David, John the Baptist, and Paul all reported similar frustrations." Then, over a period of a year, the class began keeping a list of all their prayer requests, which led them to another discovery. The majority of their petitions *were* answered! "I guess I overemphasized the requests that I thought God was ignoring, while forgetting the others," Dana concluded. His circumstances were never his chief problem after all. The real issue was *what he told himself* about them.

What about emotional complications that frequently accompany doubts, such as depression and anxiety? Again, I am not a psychologist. But Backus and Chapian address these concerns from their professional expertise, extending misbelief therapy to each topic. They explain that depression is almost always provoked by a loss of some sort (such as a person, health, or finances), after which the individual devalues him or herself, their surroundings, and/or their prospects for the future. Perhaps this is the triggering mechanism for doubting their faith, or maybe it is their faith that they think they have lost. This condition is also reported in Scripture, such as the psalmist who is cast down in Psalms 42:5–6 and 43:5.

Each situation must be placed in its proper perspective by identifying the misbeliefs. Lies might consist of telling ourselves that we cannot go on after the loss, or that the hurt itself is unbearable. Yet, many others have faced similar losses and the accompanying feelings, while continuing to lead successful lives. "Experience bears out the deception here. Many of us have told ourselves we 'cannot live without' some person, object, scheme or notion. Then this adored 'whatever' is removed from our lives and wonder of wonders, we recover" (p. 43).

The one who responds as Tracey did above, "Yes, but it's the other guy who recovers, not me," is likewise stating a misbelief. This vicious cycle must be broken. The lie needs to be identified, rejected, and replaced with the truth. A proper response might be, "Okay, I feel very bad, but this is not the end of the world," or "I've felt horrible before and, with God's assistance, I've always recovered." When a person continues reacting to a loss past a normal period of time, it is no longer the loss but the misbelief that is crippling them (p. 43).

The greatest truth we can substitute in place of depression's lies is that Christians are already both loved by God and will receive eternal blessings from him:

> . . . Christians don't have to base their worth on
> achievements or attributes. Even without any achieve-
> ments and without any special merit or attractiveness,
> the Christian can know for certain he/she is important
> and loved. Our lives have been bought and paid for
> with the blood of Jesus Christ and that means we're
> free from the pressure to *be* something, *do* something,
> *own* something, *achieve* something or *prove* something
> in order to be important and loved. We can do all these
> things or not do them and still be loved and important.
>
> Jesus loved [us] so much that He was willing to
> die on the cross so [we] could have eternal life with
> Him one day, as well as a fulfilled life here and now
> (p. 40, emphasis theirs).

Think of it: We don't have to be the best looking, the best dressed, have the best personality, or the most friends. Neither do we have to own the nicest house or car, be the best salesman or the best athlete in order to have these blessings. They belong to the believer, and they are free!

Further, *no* circumstances, pain, or loss can *ever* change these truths (Rom. 8:31–39). What an incredible blessing! Relying on God, we will never be ultimately disappointed no matter how we feel now. It is simply a fact that eternal life with the God of the universe not only outweighs *all* our present suffering and pain (Rom. 8:18), but it gives us a tremendous perspective from which to view all of our problems (2 Cor. 4:16–18).

Besides, virtually all depressed persons will recover (p. 45). So disheartened Christians can gain probable recovery now, as well as God's riches throughout eternity.

Anxiety, on the other hand, "is ordinarily defined as fear in the absence of actual danger" (p. 68). It is overestimating the likelihood of peril and exaggerating how horrible it could be. Anxiety's recurring theme is that what others think about me is of "crucial importance" to my thinking (p. 68).

As with other emotional struggles, we teach ourselves to be anxious. It is not our circumstances that create the fear—it's our own thinking about them, such as the misbelief that something "terrible" is going to happen: "What does 'terrible' mean? Usually it means something far worse than you think you can endure. You tell yourself the 'terrible' is beyond human endurance, worse than anything on earth. Truly, nothing of this sort exists" (p. 76).

Another falsehood concerns the actual likelihood of our fears becoming reality. Anxiety by its very nature generally involves imagining an evil that is actually very unlikely to occur. (How many of our worst fears throughout life have actually come to pass?) Still, the anxious person tells him or herself that this evil is unavoidable or inevitable.

We need to forcefully challenge such false beliefs with the truth that, although we may feel very bad, the horrors we are imagining have not occurred and likely won't. Even if something terrible has happened, it's not the end of a meaningful life. Believers still have the Lord, his love, and eternal life. So nothing is as terrible as we think and, while painful things do happen, believers still possess their ultimate hope. Others have lived through the same pain, and so can we, with God's help.

Conclusion

The improvement and healing of these emotional conditions frequently takes time. I have seen cases where doubting individuals have been significantly helped after just one (usually lengthy) meeting. But more often, healing the most painful effects of doubt takes practice, especially when it is ingrained in the person. Most of us have misrepresented reality to ourselves for so long that it also takes some time to cure the dilemma. Sometimes, the condition is tied so closely to our personality that, rather than a complete cure, the most we can expect is a significant lessening of the condition. Still, for this we should be thankful.

A key here, as Paul tells us in Philippians 4:9, is *repetition*. We need to *practice* the biblical remedy until it is our predominant habit. We need to be transformed by truth. The best time to fight doubt is during the suffering itself. Beyond that, we need to continue to rehearse truth as a preventive measure, even when it is not directly needed. Thus, working through our thoughts and applying truth always produces good results, even when things already seem to be going well.

As we stated in the beginning, we have made no claims that these methods are the only healing remedies. In fact, such a claim would be far from the truth. Other researchers have presented additional biblical remedies which can also lead to healing. Our next two chapters will develop other procedures. Before we move on, we need to reiterate that

Scripture does not promote a "self-help" scenario, as is so popularly declared today. Believers do not act in their own power or by the force of their own wills. The power to change our emotional doubts comes from the Lord. Paul explains at length that he had to personally learn this difficult lesson (Rom. 7:21–8:11). Yes, we are commanded to change by applying certain techniques. Yet, God is the source of our healing and true change comes by his power (Zech. 4:6).

I cannot remember anyone ever telling me, after applying the truth of Scripture, that these techniques did not either ease or heal the problem. So even if it appears that things are not getting better, we must still *repeat* the procedures, again and again if necessary. Or, as we will see in the next two chapters, we can vary the process by introducing new techniques, and try again. We often do not realize that gradual change is occurring. Perseverance and obedience lead to healing.

7

Additional Suggestions

Did you ever go through a really tough emotional time in your life while being thankful that you had already learned some major lessons that had suddenly become very helpful? It's like having the right tools in your trunk when the car breaks down. We do seem to get ample opportunities to deal with (and hopefully control) our emotions. During the years when I went through my various species of doubt, I never really had to face any serious emotional trauma at the same time. Even when I wrote my first book on doubt, I was able to do so from the intense personal experience of questioning seriously my faith for many years and of subsequently talking to dozens of others who had done the same. But I always wondered how my faith would fare in a real emergency. I got the chance to find out a few years later.

My entire life came to a screeching halt, almost like a slow motion movie, one sunny spring morning. After days of testing and comparing results, my dear wife was diagnosed with inoperable cancer. Four months later, almost to the day, she died. It was one month after our twenty-third wedding anniversary. We celebrated it while she lay in bed.

Except for two weeks in the hospital, she spent all of her last days at home, with me, our four children, and many loving relatives.

To say that it was a trying time would be the greatest of understatements. My wife and I had been exceptionally close. Amid the multiple rounds of daily feedings and medicines that had to be put through a tube, I was forced to deal not only with my own raging emotions, but also with those of our children. As time passed, friends and loved ones wanted to know how things were going, forcing me to tell the story perhaps hundreds of times.

Do biblical strategies *really* work at "crunch time," when the going is at its toughest? Can our beliefs hold firmly when what seems to be the worst possible scenarios in life are thrown at us? I thought for sure that my darkest doubts would certainly return after years of dormancy, and said so to my closest friends. But God was good and the questioning never returned. I discovered great comfort from many of the same techniques that are found in this book, especially those in the last chapter. I used them again and again, just as they are presented here. Reading and meditating on the story of Job was a special help.

I always knew these methods worked, because I had seen them in action in both my life and with others. But now I had forcibly discovered their *real* power. God's prescriptions had sustained me precisely during the time when I thought my life could hardly be more strenuous. It was an incomparably valuable lesson, taught to me under the most grueling of circumstances. God has promised that no trial or temptation will be more than we can bear (1 Cor. 10:13), and I learned that truth in a firsthand manner.

By Whose Power?

Before recommending a number of other helpful hints for dealing with emotional uncertainty, we need to repeat an important lesson from the last chapter and spend a little time explaining it further. The believer does not conquer doubt by his or her own power. Biblical suggestions for conquering worry are not to be carried out in our own strength, by somehow "hyping" ourselves to do a task by our own energy and skill. We do not pull ourselves up by our own bootstraps, so to speak. These would be *self*-help scenarios, but they are *not* what we find in Scripture.

Pete was a popular guy who was always viewed by his friends as an upbeat, optimistic person. A longtime advocate of positive thinking techniques, he seemed to have his life together. After he became a Christian, however, he reached a time of conflict. Attempting to have a consistent testimony, he began to get the impression that everything depended on his own ability to "hang in there." Avoiding sin by his own efforts and abilities especially wore him down. While he was definitely glad he had given his life to the Lord, he often wondered why his quality of life seemed to have gone down hill after his conversion. He simply grew tired of the constant effort it took to behave like a Christian.

It is true that the Bible exhorts Christians to change their ungodly behavior and embrace God's truth. The apostle James assumes that his readers have the freedom of choice to decide between God or Satan, encouraging them to submit themselves to the Lord and resist the devil (James 4:4–10). Similarly, Peter warns us to beware of the devil's tricks, so that we might resist him and stand firmly in our faith (1 Pet. 5:8–9). Persevering in the Christian faith is a popular theme in the New Testament (Heb. 10:36; 2 John 9; Rev. 22:7).

In a classic text, Paul begs his readers to offer themselves to God by revitalizing their minds, so that they will be able to know God's will (Rom. 12:1–2). Peter further encourages believers to turn from sin and crave God's path of spiritual growth (1 Pet. 2:1–3; 2 Pet. 3:18). John tells Christians that they need to obey God and walk as Jesus did (1 John 2:3–6). As believers, we are to check ourselves regularly in order to ascertain whether we are still following the Lord (1 Cor. 10:12; 11:28, 31; Gal. 6:4–5).

In each of these passages, it is assumed that believers are capable of making the appropriate decisions to turn from sin and follow God with all their hearts (Matt. 22:35–37). Accordingly, we are exhorted to give ourselves wholeheartedly to God. But it is also clear that this ability comes through God's presence in the believer's life. Paul plainly states several times that the power to conquer evil is God's, not ours (2 Cor. 4:7; 12:9–10; Eph. 6:10). Further, the weapons are God's, too (1 Cor. 10:3–5; Eph. 6:11–18). It is God's life at work within us (Gal. 2:20; Phil. 4:13). If the power, weapons, and life come from God, victory in the Christian life certainly requires his interaction with us!

Several passages include the believer's responsibility to be committed to God, as well as the divine action that is involved. One of the best known texts here is Philippians 2:12–13, where Paul tells Christians that they are to take part in working out their own salvation, only to conclude that God is the one who works it in us. While we are saved totally by God's grace rather than by our own actions, we are saved in order to do good works afterwards (Eph. 2:8–10). We shun sin by the leading and power of the Holy Spirit within us (Gal. 5:16–26). John exhorts his readers to obey God and love each other, while explaining that God lives in us, empowering us to do so (1 John. 3:23–24).

Paul leads us through the perhaps painful lesson that he learned on this subject. He had been a Pharisee with a noteworthy pedigree, even referring to himself as "a Hebrew of the Hebrews" (Phil. 3:4–6 NIV; cf. Acts 22:3–5; 26:4–11). It might have been very difficult for him not to think that, due to his credentials, he had the personal means to conquer sin in his life. But he learned that this was simply beyond his power. The things that he didn't want to do, he did; the things he wanted to do, he didn't (Rom. 7:14–25). Although there is some controversy as to whether Paul was saved during this period of failure that he describes, there is no debate that he found his victory not in his own strength, skill, and self-control, but in the victory provided by Jesus Christ (Rom. 8:1–4). It was the Holy Spirit who infused Paul with the power to defeat sin (8:5–11).

Believers are required to think and act in a responsible manner that chooses God over sin and our personal desires. We are called to radically commit our lives to our Lord. Yet, the power and weapons to do so come from God. He provides all that we need to get the job done.

How does all of this work itself out in practical terms? It seems that we are back again at our key text in Philippians 4:6–9. While Paul calls upon his readers to yield to God's truth and practice obedience, it is clear that his praise and thanksgiving are directed to God alone, both for who he is and for what he has done. He is clearly the focus of Paul's treatment, since it is through God's strength and power that the victory comes (4:13).

More Techniques

Christians need not have to figure out all the fine lines between our responsible acting and God's power. This is part of a larger theological issue that has intrigued theologians for centuries. We obviously won't solve the issues here, but for our purposes, we have said enough. That both human and divine interaction is necessary is well grounded in Scripture. Christians must decide to follow God, all the while relying on his weapons and power. The best way to do this is to apply the techniques taught in God's Word, without laboring under the delusion that we are responsible for the positive changes that occur in our lives.

In this chapter we will offer eight additional techniques that may also be applied during times of emotional doubt. Each is cognitive in nature, meaning that like the truths in Philippians 4:6–9, these are items to be integrated into our thinking. They are truths that need to be constantly considered, remembered, and meditated on, especially in worrisome times. In the next chapter, we will introduce several behavioral ingredients to fulfill Paul's exhortation that we practice God's truth. In short, biblical principles need to be *both* carefully thought through and applied.

There is no special order to the suggestions in these two chapters. The reader can pick and apply whichever recommendations are most helpful. This "mixing and matching" can be used in addition to the techniques in the last chapter, or developed into one's own pattern of thinking and acting.

(1) We need to constantly remind ourselves that emotional doubts *do not constitute any evidence against Christianity.* No matter how great our inner turmoil may be, this does not lessen the truth of biblical fact. Christianity does not hang in the balance simply because we question it. This is certainly a fact that needs to be learned and used in personal times of crisis, since the doubter often tells him or herself that the Christian faith *is* in question. We have seen that this is due to the very nature of emotional uncertainty's mood-relativity and orientation toward feelings.

In the last chapter, Shannon found this out for herself. She experienced a great victory when she realized that her moods had nothing to do with the actual state of her salvation, as she had originally feared. She had learned to concentrate instead on what God's Word told her was true.

(2) Our unedifying thoughts are often accompanied by worries and other unwanted emotions. These reactions usually do not indicate the absence of faith. Here is one of doubt's real paradoxes: *our emotions most frequently point precisely to our true faith!*

How can that possibly be? Just think about it for a minute. Unless our faith was crucially important to us, we would not react at the thought that we might not be believers. If we didn't really care, we wouldn't be upset at all. So what are our emotions saying to us? Believe it or not, they are actually dictating that we cease doubting because it hurts. Isn't that incredible? Not only has God told us in Scripture how to deal with emotional uncertainty, but he has also provided us with an early warning system that screams for attention when we disobey him!

Here is something on which we should meditate deeply. Instead of dwelling on the anxiety that we are not saved, or that Christianity is not true, we should substitute the real truth: emotional doubt usually indicates the presence of true faith. We care about our belief!

Initially, Shannon panicked when it seemed that her horrible feelings told her that she was not really saved. But later she actually rejoiced in the realization that the exact opposite was true: her emotions were in an uproar precisely because her thoughts were so contrary to her own strong Christian convictions. She was reacting, not to the true state of her heart, but to the lies she was feeding herself. This was the final nail in the coffin of her emotional doubt. She was saved—and cured!

(3) When suffering through emotional doubt, a very helpful technique is to *minimize the problem without neglecting its correction.* In other words, it is beneficial to remember and concentrate on the fact that many others have faced what you have or suffered similar obstacles (1 Cor. 10:13). You are not alone in this. Doubt is common to human beings in general. This is not an excuse to treat religious uncertainty lightly, but knowing that others are also struggling with it somehow has the effect of allowing us to relax a bit (cf. 1 Pet. 5:9).

Years ago I was teaching a seminary class that attempted to apply apologetic principles to ministry. One of the assignments required the students to find someone who was doubting and attempt to counsel them through it. One student discovered an example of how truth-telling can heal. He reported that the doubter he worked with (a fellow seminary student) was so amazed to find that fellow Christians also

frequently questioned their faith that this fact alone brought him substantial relief. It led, in turn, to another liberating thought: the original
problem was emotional in nature and needed to be treated as such, not
as some deep-seated spiritual dilemma.

(4) Anxiety during doubt is frequently *short-lived*. In cases of
worry, one helpful technique is to remind ourselves that the fear or
other negative feelings need not last very long.

Once Philip realized this truth, he confronted his customary fear by
forcefully declaring to himself, "Just calm down. Relax! This will only
last a little while." Then he projected his thoughts to an hour or so in
the future, and pictured being calm and restful. He experienced peace
almost immediately. Each time he did this, he was able to sit back and
watch as the levels on his "doubt barometer" dropped. As with some
medical prescriptions, he repeated the dose whenever needed. He found
that once he had taken the edge off his unruly emotions, it became
much easier to apply other principles to deal with the fear itself, which
was now declining even more quickly.

(5) When suffering in the grips of acute emotional doubt, another
remedy will perhaps give the fastest relief: *change the subject quickly,
forcefully, and completely*. The sufferer should concentrate his or her
attention on another topic altogether. One of the methods we've already
mentioned should suffice, such as prayer, thanksgiving, praise, or
addressing our lies directly. There are other ways to alter your thoughts
too: think about a joyous occasion of the past, or look forward to a
future vacation or holiday with loved ones. Concentrate for a few minutes on specific details. Basically, any change of subject usually lessens
the worry levels.

Or you might wish to try a behavioral alternative, like calling a friend
on the phone, jogging, walking, biking, or swimming. The latter methods
are best seen as Band-Aids™ in the sense that, while they don't heal the
problem, they can temporarily ease the pain, and often quite quickly.

Alexis was close to a panic attack as her uncontrollable thoughts were attacking her faith once again. Would she ever get a handle on these doubts? And they hurt so much—absolutely anything was preferable to these awful feelings! Soon she was pacing, spinning rapidly on her heel, and starting back in the other direction. Her pulse and breathing had both increased dramatically. Would she find relief?

When the telephone rang, Alexis ran to pick up the receiver. It was her best friend with news about last night's blind date. Two minutes into the conversation, Alexis rather absent mindedly remembered that she had not been feeling well. But now she felt fine! Later reflection brought a flood of lessons to Alexis' mind. She was simply amazed at how quickly the panic had subsided. One minute it was there, and the next minute it wasn't! Additionally, she realized rather sheepishly that she wasn't dying, as she was beginning to think during the attack. "I'll have to remember that trick next time," she told herself lightheartedly, cringing slightly at the thought that the feeling might return.

Over time, Alexis also realized that the intruding thoughts were not as uncontrollable as she had thought. After all, a rather minor interruption was all it took! And the worries weren't the unbearable horrors she had thought they were. She had lived to tell about it, hadn't she? All of this from a simple phone call!

(6) *Don't argue with yourself concerning the factual grounds for Christianity during an attack of anxious doubt.* Commonly, when one mistakenly identifies emotional questioning as being factual in nature, the doubter often resorts to arguing the evidential basis for Christianity, falsely concluding that this will cause the emotions to retreat. But as we've said many times, emotional doubts are not usually corrected by factual recitations. Thus, pulling the facts out at this point will allow them only to be colored in one's mind by the emotional element. Although it may be tough to admit, when our emotions go to war against our reason, the emotions usually win. So why invite disaster?

Here someone may raise the question, "Hey, wait a minute. You've said many times that we *should* argue during our episodes of doubt. So why shouldn't we do it here?" This observation is correct, but the distinction lies in the *nature* of the arguing. Facts are used with factual doubts, while cognitive and behavioral techniques are used with emotional questioning. These latter grounds should be argued immediately. But since facts seldom end the emotional doubt, we shouldn't cross that line. There is plenty of time to return later to the evidences for Christianity, after one is calm, but not before then.

(7) During attacks of emotional doubt, *it is helpful to continue affirming our belief in the Lord.* When our faith is being assailed, we should concentrate on trusting God, regardless of the circumstances.

Is a man considered a good friend or a poor one if he gives up on his best buddy as soon as a stranger challenges him? How about our faithful commitment to a spouse during a tough time? In the same way, why should we deny Jesus when our emotions question him? People are not the same as ideas, and therefore require greater allegiance. Christians need to affirm their allegiance to their Lord.

(8) *Pick a biblical hero who went through tough times*—like Job, Abraham, Moses, David, Daniel, John the Baptist, or Paul, and let their life speak to you. Study their situations carefully and recall both their struggles and their victories. Why was Job satisfied without ever learning why he suffered? How did Abraham overcome his lack of faith so that he became known as the man of faith? Why were the psalmists content even when God was silent? How did Jesus treat the emotional doubts John the Baptist suffered while he was isolated in prison? What other problems were faced by these saints? How did they deal with them? Did they achieve victory immediately? What did they learn from these conflicts?

Then consider what you can learn today from their past struggles. What are the parallels? Did they suffer pain, as we do today? Is our faith sometimes as weak? Do we wonder why our prayers are not always answered the way we think they should be? Are we ever isolated, without Christian fellowship? What effect does all of this have on our emotions? How can we draw strength from these biblical testimonies? Can we also make a similar move from the problem to the solution? Concentrate on these issues and take note of some biblical lessons that might be learned and applied.

Hopefully, at least a few of these additional suggestions will be beneficial in combating emotional uncertainty. I would suggest trying each one during worrisome moments and utilizing those that show the most promise.

Conclusion

Christians are continually exhorted throughout Scripture to resist the devil and shun sin. We are also told to follow God with all of our hearts. All of this only makes sense if we have some responsibility in the process. But we are additionally told that it is God's power, weapons, and his indwelling of believers that produces the victory. We must decide to follow him and apply the techniques that he commands, yet do so in his strength.

So how did Pete resolve his dilemma about reacting to life in his own strength? It took a while, but he learned that Christianity is not about working oneself up into a frenzy in order to obey a list of dos and don'ts. Rather, it is an integrated lifestyle that allows God to work through the believer so that they actually *prefer* to make the choices they should. Thus, Pete felt liberated when he learned that the Christian faith is more about exuberant, committed living in light of eternity than it is about always having a burden to react against everything.

For most believers, the problem does not come from any lack of conviction that they need to do something. After all, they are in pain!

They desire remedies that work. The question concerns which techniques best treat their specific form of doubt and how these should be exercised, especially during times of struggle. Applying the truth is perhaps the most crucial decision they will make on this subject.

Hopefully, the suggested cognitive procedures in the last two chapters will provide some thoughtful sorts of consolation. In the next chapter we will turn to behavioral changes that also address our emotional struggles with faith.

Practice! Practice! Practice!

Seldom have I experienced anything more marvelous than watching someone who has suffered grievously from the effects of religious doubt "catch on" to the appropriate techniques. For those who learn and continually practice biblical prescriptions, even when their situations look bleak and involve an exceptional amount of work, fantastic blessings can result. Two cases, in particular, come to my mind.

When Missy came to talk with me, she seemed to be suffering from more than the ordinary sort of emotional doubt. I sent her to a counseling clinic, where she was diagnosed with a potentially serious psychological disorder. She was treated with medicine and released, but she still had to deal with what she was telling herself concerning her salvation.

We met many times while she attempted to grasp the essentials of assurance. Meanwhile, many other painful things were going on in Missy's life, too. There were multiple symptoms with which to deal. For several months there were ups and downs. Sometimes things were better, other times they were not. But very slowly she began to progress. The more she practiced, the stronger she got.

Due to the complicated nature of her situation, far beyond the emotional doubt alone, Missy needed some time to work everything through. At first, she failed to apply the principles in Philippians 4:6–9 in any consistent manner. But later it was these very precepts, in particular, that really changed her life.

Twelve years later, it is apparent that the change has lasted for the long term, as well. A few conversations have shown that she no longer struggles with the issues that had dominated her life. Although her path didn't always travel a straight line upwards, and there were trials along the way, the trip ended with a fantastic victory. The principles she had learned affected more than just her doubt. They became beacons for her life, as she applied them to other subjects, too. Today, Missy is a missionary in Eastern Europe, sharing her testimony with other hurting people.

The second case came fairly early in my growing number of instructional sessions with doubters. It involved a graduate student, James, who repeatedly and sometimes belligerently charged God with not loving him. No amount of discussion would cause him to think otherwise. Some rather serious child abuse, along with some even more dangerous medical problems that altered moods, added much to his doubts.

We talked frequently about his questioning, our meetings often taking the form of his challenging me to convince him that the biblical methods would work. Many a morning I would round the last corner to my office, only to find him sitting there without an appointment, wanting me to address his needs right then and there. Calls at home, or impromptu meetings at sporting events for more discussions, were commonplace. All during this time, James steadfastly refused to even try to apply the biblical principles. In short order, I was worn out!

One night James came to a college game to talk because he knew I would be there. It had taken a long time for me to get to this place, but I had finally had enough. I told him that he and I were going to duck into the first place we could find after the game, where I was going to repeat the principles to him one more time. If he didn't make any more effort to apply them than he had done in the previous few weeks, we were done talking. That meeting after the game seemed to be the turning point! He was a very intelligent man and he certainly knew the proper responses to his doubt. Now he began to practice them, and he made very rapid progress.

Several months later, James and I had lunch together. He was telling me how well he was doing, when a young lady came over and asked if she could sit and talk for a few minutes about her problems with doubt. Imagine my surprise when, before I could respond to the problem she had outlined, James held up his hand.

"May I handle this one?" he asked me. Dumbfounded, I sat quietly and listened, realizing that I might have to jump in at any moment in order to rescue the woman from who-knew-what-kind of advice! To my utter astonishment, James made a flawless case for beating emotional doubt. The woman walked away encouraged!

James' changed life has also stood the test of time. He, too, had a tough "row to hoe," largely due to the outside factors mentioned above. In fact, he even needed surgery to correct some of the damage of the child abuse he had withstood. But now, fourteen years later, he is doing magnificently. There are no traces of the radical version of emotional doubt that had afflicted him, all due, he has said, to his finally beginning to practice principles like Paul's in Philippians 4:6–9. He has since matured into a strong Christian leader, and is today pastoring a thriving church.

What else can we say? God changes the lives of those who practice his principles!

Resisting the Practice of God's Truth

Why did both Missy and James drag their heels so much when provided with a remedy to their emotional doubt? Both were suffering a significant amount of pain. Their problems were affecting every aspect of their lives. Doesn't it seem that they would jump at the opportunity to get some relief? So why did they refuse to act for such a long time? For that matter, why does anyone fail to apply God's truth when they have come to the end of themselves? There are few more intriguing subplots involved in this topic. In my experience, the two most difficult points in the entire process of dealing with emotional doubt is discovering the falsehoods we tell ourselves and implementing God's truth. It seems especially tough to do the latter precisely during the time in which we are most in need. These are the subjects for this chapter.

Of course, the bottom line for not applying truth is always the same: we prefer our ways to God's ways. It's easy to spot this in cases involving unbelievers (Rom. 1:18–32). But as we saw in the last chapter, believers, too, struggle with disobeying God even after we know his will (James. 4:1–10; 1 Pet. 2:1–3).

Given that even believers ignore God's teachings and disobey him, why, more specifically, might a Christian fail to apply God's directives concerning their emotional doubt, when they are so obviously hurting and obedience might render relief? One reason is that it is difficult to pinpoint our own unedifying thoughts. After all, why would we ever want to lie to ourselves? Yet, God has forewarned us that it is very difficult to know our own hearts, and why we do the things we do (Jer. 17:9). It would seem that we are all candidates for unintentionally misdirecting ourselves.

Another major reason we miss the untruths we tell ourselves is that we think there is actually some truth to them. I hear this reasoning quite frequently: "Well, didn't I just flunk my big exam?" or "Isn't it true that

I was just diagnosed with a very serious illness?" When you hear it for the first time, this complaint really does sound like a showstopper. What if the worst thing *has* just happened?

When partial truth is mixed in with untruth, the doubting individual is often tempted to wonder if our biblical procedure for relief really works at all. This sort of case is more difficult to work through, specifically because the person is less likely to see that they are still repeating untruths. Since the misbeliefs are present along with some truth, the former must be corrected if we are to achieve victory over our emotional questions. After all, it is the mistaken portion of the belief that causes the harm. The hidden lies that often rear their heads in these circumstances are more elusive due to the fact that the negative event has already occurred. Frequently I hear: "Because of these horrible things, my life is forever ruined. I'll never be the same." "My anxiety is completely justified, due to the hurt in my life. My circumstances have caused all of this." "The worst thing possible has just happened to me."

But our lives should not revolve around half-truths or temporary truths. Even though something "bad" has happened, it is the unnoticed misbelief that causes the anxiety. In cases like these, the half-truth hurts more than the outright lie.

Once, after I lectured on this subject, Chuck came up to me to talk. He had just lost his job and was in a state of turmoil. A perceptive man, he discovered that he was more prone to question God's goodness now: "How could God really love me?" Granted, this was a serious predicament for him and his family. But while losing his job was definitely significant, it was also temporary. In no sense was it the worst thing that could possibly happen to Chuck. Unfortunately, he told himself that it was just that: unbearable.

In situations like Chuck's, it's not the lost job that trips people up and causes the pain. If you still question this statement, then think about this: How can losing a job make us jump to the conclusion that

God has done something to us, or abandoned us, *unless* we're drawing conclusions *from* the event itself? The problem is what we tell ourselves *about* losing the job: "I'll probably never be happy again." "We'll have to move and the kids will hate it." "Even if I do get another job, it'll be for less money." "We'll have to change our lifestyle." "I won't like the job as much." "God doesn't care about my family."

After giving him a list like this one, I asked Chuck if he ever said things like this to himself. He admitted that he had.

In other words, the chief obstacle with half-true statements is that the false portion will work on us, frequently causing anxious doubt. Like an undetected physical sickness, the lie stays hidden behind the partial truth until it is strong enough to produce some harm. By then, it is much more troublesome to remove.

Still another reason that we fail to apply God's truth to our doubt is that it may not be pleasant. Like pulling weeds, losing weight, or having a cavity filled, the final results might be quite nice, but we can never quite get around to performing the difficult procedure. Ridding our lives of doubt is admittedly not as simple as taking two aspirins and going to bed. God has told us that we must be willing to follow the instructions; in other words, we must be active participants. Especially since the remedy is best applied during the problem (like medicine), this adds to the uncomfortable nature of the healing process. Anxiety is tough enough by itself without us having to do something else amid the turmoil. It's like crying out: "Just leave me alone with my worry!" We would rather procrastinate than face the music.

There are still other reasons that sometimes figure in when someone exhibits a problem with emotional doubt, but fails to take positive steps about it. Some just don't get the point and, in spite of all indications to the contrary, still think that circumstances directly cause the emotions. Other doubters prefer the process of counseling more than they wish to be healed. Perhaps craving either attention or friendship, curing the uncertainty would effectively cut the counselor-client relationship short. Others cannot admit that they have a problem because that would militate against their sense of spiritual well-being or personal worth. It is far easier to deny the problem altogether or to place the blame elsewhere—probably on the offending events or persons.

At any rate, there comes a time when doubters must make a choice. No one else can tackle their questioning for them. But the good news is that there is a remedy that works. It just needs to be applied.

When Should We Practice?

There is no substitute for *practice*. With all diligence, we should exchange our anxious doubts for God's glorious truths. God's peace has been promised to us.

We have said that the most difficult time in which to implement God's instructions is *during* the period of doubting, since it sometimes takes an extraordinary effort to change subjects when our thinking is dominated by the painful dilemma itself. But this is also when we most need to apply God's strategies. It is precisely *because* we are changing the subject that the quandary subsides. It's like taking medicine: it might not taste good, but we require it most when we are sick. Like digging for splinters in a child's hand, temporary pain is the way to gain lasting relief!

So the onset of the condition is the signal for action. Load the cannons and begin the assault! If healing and spiritual growth are desired, then we have to be willing to pay the price. Who knows? The solution may even be easier than expected, especially after some initial healing occurs. Like going home, when familiar territory comes into view, we are more willing to push ourselves.

I think the application comes much more easily to those who are willing to force their way doggedly toward the finish line. In this chapter,

I've used examples from those who had lengthy healing processes. But it need not be that way. I've seen far more cases where the individual was almost completely healed of the more painful elements of their doubt by a concentrated application over a short period of time.

The chief idea here is to practice God's truths, and to do so particularly during the roughest times. The truth should be applied whether we feel like it or not. Paul tells us in Philippians 4:9 that rehearsing proper thinking until it becomes a habit is one of the keys to achieving peace.

We have already said that preventive therapy is also important. Like taking vitamins or participating in an exercise program, preparation ahead of time can be very helpful. As we get vaccinated during healthy times, so doubt prevention furnishes the necessary means to equip us for future needs, perhaps even keeping that rough time from coming altogether. Certainly, it often lessens the force of the emotional storm.

The main target audience for this strategy is those who know they have a tendency towards doubting. For this group of individuals, thinking through the options ahead of time allows them to greet the presence of questioning with the response, "Oh, you again. I've been waiting for you!"

What Should We Practice?

In the last two chapters, we focused on a number of cognitive practices that provide us with ammunition against doubt. Here we will provide seven behavioral techniques that address Paul's command to continually *rehearse* truth until it becomes a way of life (Phil. 4:9). Once again, the doubter may pick and choose methods that best meet his or her particular needs. Since each of the suggestions is biblical, applying any of them will be a positive step.

(1) **Pray through the doubt.** Paul (Phil. 4:6) and Peter (1 Pet. 5:7) both command prayer during troubled times. Our petitions should be specific. While this is a great privilege, Scripture speaks of conditions

for God's answers. We are told to confess our sins beforehand (Ps. 66:18), exercise faith (Mark 11:24; James. 1:5–8), be obedient to him (John 15:7; 1 John 3:22), and pray according to God's will (1 John 5:14–15) in Jesus' name (John 14:13–14; 15:16).

To turn the cognitive exercise of prayer into a behavioral one, several things could be done. We could write out our prayer requests, as well as the results. One helpful way is to list the specific requests in the left-hand margin, the results in a middle column, and any special notations on the right side of the sheet. As with Dana and his Sunday school class in chapter 6, this exercise could even be done with others. Answers are usually an encouragement to everyone's faith and serve as a preventative measure against the common form of doubt that questions God's involvement in our lives.

I kept a list of prayer requests and answers over a period of about two years. During that time, approximately two out of three prayers were answered. Some of these were of the very difficult (even "impossible") variety, and to my surprise, most of those received positive responses. Later, a seminary student told me that, his Sunday school class, like Dana's, also made a record of their classroom requests. Interestingly, they came up with a very similar result—about 70 percent of their prayers were answered.

We could also share with others in corporate prayer times, not only petitioning aloud, but rejoicing in the answers, too. I have often said that one of the main things I would emphasize if I ever returned to the pastorate would be the answers God sends, as well as the actual prayer requests. This is a tremendous encouragement to all believers, but seems often to be neglected.

(2) **Meditate through the doubt.** Many times in Scripture, believers are told to meditate on God's truth (about a dozen times in Ps. 119 alone). As opposed to the Eastern view of emptying the mind, biblical meditation is thinking deeply and single mindedly on God's truth. We've

already mentioned briefly some examples of content in discussing Paul's exhortation in Philippians 4:8.

Meditation is a wonderful cognitive avenue by which to deal with particular cases of doubt, as well as practice doubt prevention. During many of my doubting years, I made more use of this method than at any other time. Sitting on my porch on a dark, starry evening, I worked through various problematic issues, one by one. Usually, my chief methods were going through either Philippians 4:6–9 or Backus and Chapian's three stages, step by step. It's a great way to think about God's truth, as Paul commands.

But meditation can also be practiced corporately (Ps. 48:9; 63:2), as a behavioral technique. It can be a public exercise for believers who, together, concentrate on the Lord's truths, perhaps centered around a particular theme. In a corporate setting, strength can be drawn from sharing these thoughts together, too.

(3) **Worship through the doubt.** We've discussed Paul's exhortation to practice both thanksgiving for God's blessings and praise for his character. These two methods are especially helpful during times of uncertainty. Thanking and praising, in a very special way, liberate the believer to look beyond his or her immediate problems toward God. It is very difficult to practice either one and yet remain engulfed in one's troubles.

A behavioral component can be easily constructed here. We could compose our own psalm unto the Lord. Whether or not you consider yourself a poet, share your deepest words of adoration with your God. Say them aloud. Or, sit on your porch on a still morning during sunrise and sing praises to God. What is your favorite hymn or praise chorus? Perhaps you would prefer to go for a walk and say or sing your words of praise.

Further, it is crucial to attend a Bible-believing church that takes worship seriously, where the emphasis is on meeting with God in fellowship with others of like mind. The corporate element adds a spark to our personal adoration.

(4) **Memorize through the doubt.** Take note of your most bothersome doubts. Which verses best apply to them? Which biblical truths most apply to your misbeliefs? How can you think more clearly about them? Write or type each text on a note card, arrange them in a meaningful order, and keep them together.

For years I carried with me, everywhere I went, a small container of business cards on which I wrote the truths that I most needed to be reminded of. I read them so much that the edge of every card became tattered and worn. Sometimes I tired of seeing the same verses as I flipped through them, so I repeatedly told myself, "Yes, I know that." But then my efforts against the doubts would stagnate. On one of the days when I thought I was making too little progress, I wrote across the bottom of one card: "If you *know* it, then *do* it!" Sometimes we need less knowledge and more practice!

(5) **Journal through the doubt.** Keep a diary of your daily spiritual walk with the Lord. What doubts plagued you today? What things happened to you that you might have interpreted negatively, providing the stimulus for these thoughts? How did you respond to them? What methods worked? Which ones did not work so well? Could you have reacted in ways that would have been more profitable? What did you learn about God's truth and its application? A chart might be helpful. Please add words.

Then periodically go back through previous days and see if you have made any progress. Do you notice any trends? Overall, do you find yourself returning to certain methods over others? Many believers have gained major insights into their walk with the Lord by taking the time to record thoughts and ideas like these.

(6) **Recall through the doubt.** Many biblical texts encourage believers to review past history in order to see what God has done (Ps. 105; 106; 114). In the last chapter, I suggested an exercise of picking a biblical hero or two who underwent doubt, in order to learn from their

trials. As an additional exercise, make a list of their problems, their circumstances, how they responded to them, and how it all turned out.

Another sort of recall is to count the answers to prayer that we have received over a specific period of time. Write them down. Meditate on the things God has done in your life. How many times have you triumphed due to his goodness? How does this show that he is active in your life today? During times when I have questioned God's involvement, this method has never failed to be a ready antidote.

(7) **Talk through the doubt.** With emotional doubts, few things are as helpful as having a close friend or relative assist us in picking out our misbeliefs. Of course, the helper has to understand the "system," so clue them in and watch this technique work. Loved ones often see the improper things we tell ourselves, even when we do not. Time and time again I've known the informed friend to notice what the doubter didn't. Additionally, not only is the method readily available, but it can be a forceful change of subject, as we saw with Alexis in chapter 7. It is for this very reason that I often encourage a counselee to bring such a friend to the initial meeting, so they can learn the methods together.

Wendy discovered that it was quite difficult for her to recognize her own distortions of the truth, since she had been believing these unedifying thoughts for so long. Frequently she let things pass that she should have caught. But on one occasion, her close friend Amber happened to ask her why she had just made a certain comment. Recognizing that this was one of the things she had been working on, but had missed, Wendy explained the basic principles of Philippians 4 to her roommate. After that, Amber began to help Wendy uncover her falsehoods. Together they labored to weed out these untruths. Wendy even found a few of Amber's problem areas, too!

Conclusion

Through all of our cognitive tools and behavior changes, we need to remember that victory rests chiefly in God's power, weapons, and indwelling. Explaining our predicament to God and giving it over to him, while at the same time expressing our faith in him regardless of whether or not we obtain immediate answers, are moves in the right direction. They help us to reaffirm our reliance on God, even when the way ahead is not clear. This is one way to strengthen our faith.

Unfortunately, when we believe our own lies, we also fail to look beyond our immediate circumstances. But temporal matters, even when truthful, are different from ultimate truth. In contrast, Christians should be most concerned about ultimate truth. We need to obey our Lord and lay up treasures in heaven, just as Jesus instructed us to do (Matt. 6:19–34). One truth to continually drive home is that, even when Christians flunk big exams or think that God did not answer their prayer, they still have eternal life. They should view the present in light of their eternal future. If believers cannot appreciate the force of this, it could be because they have not really struggled with their salvation.

Here is the major point: Christians do not have to pass exams, keep their jobs, or even have the most successful prayer lives in order to be saved. Neither do they have to be the most popular, the best dressed, or the best athletes in the world. They don't even have to be able to handle their doubt well! In fact, they do not have to do or be anything, except believers in Jesus Christ, in order to have the ultimate blessing of eternal life.

It is from this eternal perspective that all other problems should be viewed. Even death itself is not the definitive issue; that distinction belongs to the priority of God and his kingdom (Matt. 6:33). This is the ultimate truth to be practiced.

9

Living with Questions

In the process of addressing emotional doubt, we have raised another question that is so large that it demands a separate treatment. Actually, few subjects raise more doubts than this one, and to get over this problem would bring relief to many believers. How can we be content in our Christian lives even though we may still have many unanswered questions? And how do we face the fact that many brothers and sisters in Christ differ from us in some rather important areas of theology?

Ken was obviously flustered by this whole issue. No, this is a rather glaring understatement. He was absolutely at his wits' end when he called me from his Midwest church where he had become a very successful pastor. Even though he had never been my student, I was lumped in with his seminary professors.

"You guys taught us theology," Ken accused, "as if all evangelicals believe the same thing. But I've discovered that they don't. In fact, they're quite different." Then he dropped the bombshell: "I've just about come to think that theology is all a matter of interpretation."

Although he didn't say it, he then implied that he was considering leaving the pastorate because of this conclusion!

"Wow!" I said. "All of this simply from discovering different expressions of theology among believers?"

Ken and I talked for some time. I was reminded that an area that had never really been a concern to me in my doubting days did plague many Christians. But why would someone take the conclusion in the direction of Ken's radical stance? I couldn't fathom how he could get where he was for those reasons.

A second example came some years later. One of my students in a doctoral class, Gene, was a pastor who had struggled with some similar issues. He came up to me privately and thanked me profusely for the discussion. For years he had been bothered by a particular doctrinal attitude that was not even taught in the Bible! His consternation had come from feeling that he needed to take the company line on a perspective that he never personally believed. But his questions caused him to have doubts, wondering if he was some sort of hypocrite because he didn't support the status quo of his denomination.

Why do Christians seem so puzzled when they encounter other believers from a slightly different perspective than their own? And how should we handle the special sort of doubt that often results?

Why Are There Theological Differences?

Why are there major distinctions between religious denominations? Why have Bible-believing theologians through the centuries struggled over enduring questions, like the sovereignty of God, the free will of created persons, the perseverance of the saints, the sign gifts, or the age of the earth? How should we respond when we think we have solved one of these issues for ourselves, only to discover that there are equally well-meaning Christians who do not agree? Further, what do we do when careful study does *not* reveal an answer, including the quandary of simply not knowing why certain things happen the way they do?

I think one reason these scenarios especially plague Christians is that many of our leaders teach that *all* truth can be known *absolutely*. In no uncertain terms, they imply (if not directly teach) that their interpretation of a particular doctrine is the *only* possible position on the topic. In short, truth is what they say it is.

This at least adds to the confusion, if not being a chief reason for it. Obviously, if I (along with a few buddies who agree with me) am the sole arbiter of truth, but there are other true believers who disagree, then someone is clearly wrong. Unfortunately, the issue is often solved by imperial edict: "I am your leader and I am right. If you want the truth you'll listen to me." This sort of attitude just adds to the conflict, as well as to the sensitive believer's doubt.

So, if the Bible is the inspired Word of God, then why should you believe one thing, while I believe another? Is Ken right—is it all just a matter of interpretation? Why are there so many differences and denominations? Let's begin by noting a few reasons why this there are different outlooks among Christians.

Some denominational differences are not theological, but political, social, or even geographical. Historical surveys will show that theologically similar groups were formed either before they came to America, or originated many years ago in different areas of the country. Others share similar theological stances, but tend toward varying political and social views. Social status can account for other differences. Unfortunately, too many deviations are related more to power struggles, church splits, and leadership influence than to biblical interpretation.

Closely aligned with these reasons are changes in the body of Christ over two thousand years which have developed into doctrinal discussions at levels beyond what is encountered in Scripture. Dozens of cultural, racial, world religious, missionary, and other theological situations have pushed Christians to make distinctions that sometimes go beyond what we are told about these issues in Scripture.

Further, virtually everyone experiences some sort of doubt and disagreement simply because we are human beings. We have said that the root cause of our uncertainty is our sin nature. While this does not mean that all doubt is necessarily sin, it does imply that many of our differences are due to the fact that we are finite persons. Questions arise simply because, by nature, we don't know all the answers. Yet, we sometimes respond by dogmatically asserting what we don't know!

These initial responses can explain a fair amount of the theological differences among believers. But they do not explain them all. Our last answer will probably shock many readers: The Bible itself simply does not always clarify every conceivable question.

But, who says Scripture has to clear up every doctrinal matter? Is it possible that there are many things that God simply didn't want to tell us? If this is so, much of our confusion would then come from our attempting to force issues and place God's truth within certain boundaries. Admittedly it is inviting, to say the least, to think that we have been given the keys to all theological truth. That would be just like humans, wouldn't it—to take dogmatic stands on subjects when we don't have enough information to make these judgments?

I think there is clear biblical precedent for this view. Job concluded that he knew enough about God to trust him in those areas that he didn't understand (Job 42:1–6). Remember, Job never received an answer from the Lord concerning the reason for his suffering, yet he trusted and was blessed. Why? Scripture tells us that God's ways are not the same as ours, but higher (Isa. 55:8–9). How many times throughout history has God not explained a similar question to a hurting believer?

Let me take a further step—and perhaps a startling one. I think the New Testament provides other examples where certain areas were *purposely* left unresolved. One excellent instance is a topic that is in the forefront of current discussions—the time of Jesus Christ's return for his church. In answer to his disciples' question (Mark 13:3–4), our Lord warned that not even he knew the time for this event, that they only needed to remain alert and ready (13:32–37). Later the disciples asked again, and again they heard the same answer—God the Father was the sole authority on this subject, and he alone knew the time of the end (Acts 1:6–7).

But Christians today repeatedly qualify Jesus' remarks so that, while we don't know the *exact* moment of his return, we presume to know at least the decade! Believers have been responding this way for centuries, contrary to Jesus' admonitions to make sure that we are anticipating his return *without* worrying about the timing. That knowledge has simply not been given to us.

There are also examples where clear directions are not given for everyday living. The Bible even indicates that it is permissible for Christians to hold differing viewpoints on certain personal, ethical, or theological subjects, without the biblical writer resolving those differences for us. Take the personal argument between Paul and Barnabas for instance. The quarrel was so sharp that the two missionaries split up (Acts 15:36–41). It would seem from Luke's choice of words in verse 39 that the matter was rather heated. Of course, it might just be concluded that this was a clash of personalities that is inevitable whenever human beings work together long enough, and that would be fair. But we still don't want to miss the obvious point: apparently, either Paul or Barnabas was ultimately "right" or "wrong." As Luke did not try to decide this issue, neither should we jump in and try to resolve the conflict, as we attempt to do with so many other issues!

Yet there are other biblical instances when there were clashes between early Christians, with verdicts being given. The dispute regarding observance of the law, between Paul and Peter, contained a personal element, as well as theological roots. Finally, Paul ended the debate by declaring that Peter was wrong (Gal. 2:11–14)! Scholars disagree whether Acts 15:1–35 and Galatians 2:1–10 describe the same occasion, so here are potentially two situations where the issue of law observance brought about an early apostolic assembly to decide the nature of the gospel. In both texts, Paul was vindicated.

In Romans 14:1–4, the same apostle who disagreed with Barnabas and announced Peter's error turned to ethical differences between early believers *without* casting any blame. In fact, he specifically tells his readers *not* to pass judgment in certain disputes, like that of diet, saying that both he who eats meat and he who does not is accepted by God (14:4b, 6b, 10). Similarly, Paul addressed the question of eating meat offered to idols by declaring that the one who refuses to eat is no better off than the one who eats (1 Cor. 8:7–8; cf. 1 Cor. 10:25–30).

But personal and ethical issues are not the only ones on which Paul fails to take sides. He also addressed a topic of crucial theological significance in the early church—that of the observance of special days. Paul probably had in mind here the earthshaking subject of sabbath observance, which split Gentile and Jewish believers. Once again, he judged that there is room for differing convictions (Rom. 14:5–6, 10). This is really an incredible conclusion in light of Paul's comments elsewhere that the observance of special days may indicate that a person is no longer following the path of God's grace (Gal. 4:10–11; cf. 3:1–3). Perhaps the key here is that Paul thought Jewish believers had an option that Gentile believers, who don't obey the Jewish law, didn't have. But in Romans 14:5b, he allows everyone to be persuaded by their own convictions, without any absolute commands.

But amid the freedom that believers have on such matters (Gal. 2:4; 1 Cor. 10:30), Paul still cautions us not to be stumbling blocks to weaker believers. If others are bothered by our actions, we should refrain from pursuing our will when we are with them (1 Cor. 8:9–13; 10:23–33). All believers should work for the same purposes, to bring people to Christ and to edify believers (1 Cor. 3:1–9, 22–23; 10:23–24, 31–33). So we may have to subject our freedom to our ministry objectives.

In sum, our last reason for the presence of differences among believers is that not all issues—personal, ethical, or even doctrinal—can be figured out (as with Job's lesson about God's sovereignty or the time of Jesus' return), or decided in strict terms (as with the various issues mentioned by Paul). Our conclusion, therefore, is that we have created yet another false belief here! While some Christians seem to think that biblical theology and other issues are *always* knowable in concrete terms, this is plainly not the case. So why do we finite beings beat ourselves (and others) trying to figure out all theological and other matters?

Since we are human beings, questioning to one extent or another will probably always be part of our lifelong experience. So get used to it! We should not attempt to reach some sort of utopia in this life, where there are no more uncertainties. They will always be present with us. But these need not be the same as doubts. One important question, then, is how we should differentiate those matters that we will not always know and shouldn't try to hammer out from those that we must know in order to be orthodox believers. This is a crucial distinction. Maybe we will find some concealed blessings along the way—some personal freedom and a new appreciation of others in the body of Christ with whom we do not agree on one hundred percent of all issues.

Differentiating Theology

One way to answer the critical question concerning Christianity's unnegotiable areas of theology is to distinguish between beliefs that are absolutely indispensable and those that invite further research. But how do we do this? What are the parameters for such a study?

There are several methods to help us establish our fundamental beliefs. Crucial doctrines that are foundational to Christianity have at least four characteristics: (1) they are clearly taught in Scripture; (2) they are identified as being centrally important; (3) there are strong evidences for each (as we saw in chapter 5); and (4) they occur prominently in classic statements of faith down through the ages. Therefore, all fundamental doctrines should figure both *clearly* and *prominently* in Scripture, and be supported strongly in terms of both *apologetics* and *church history.*

At the head of the list belongs the content of the gospel. What is the absolute minimum "truth" that makes up the heart of the Christian faith? When Paul defines his central message, there are three doctrines that are repeated each time: the deity, death, and resurrection of Jesus. A person is saved by exercising faith in the person of Jesus Christ in light of these truths (Rom. 10:9; 1 Cor. 15:3–4; 2 Tim. 2:8–9). Other items are also mentioned in various texts, but it appears that these three are the only ones always included without exception.

Besides the core of the gospel, other fundamental doctrines that fulfill our four criteria include the belief in one God (Deut. 6:4) in three separate persons (Eph. 4:4–6); creation (Gen. 1:1–3; Col. 1:16); the inspiration of Scripture (2 Tim. 3:16; 2 Pet. 1:21); the virgin birth (Matt. 1:18–23) and incarnation of Jesus Christ (John 1:14); his second coming (Acts 1:9–11; Rev. 1:7); the sinful nature of human beings (Rom. 3:23; 6:23); eternal life for believers (John 6:47; 14:1–4); and eternal judgment for unbelievers (Dan. 12:2; Matt. 25:41–46).

There is widespread agreement among orthodox believers on at least the general contours of these doctrines, and especially concerning faith in the Jesus Christ of the New Testament gospel. This is the case whatever the specific Christian denomination. Disagreements and distinctives usually come in less crucial areas.

One way to discern the difference between absolutely crucial matters of theology and secondary ones is to ask whether one's beliefs on either side of the issue would threaten the essence of the Christian faith. The vast majority of the most heated disputes among Christians would cause absolutely no change to ultimate truth. They are lesser problems that we must not allow to prey on our emotions because they do not actually affect our faith *whatever* the view taken. (Obviously, someone could still take one of these non-fundamental options to a ridiculous point. We will not address that here.)

There are numerous examples of hot issues that do not affect the central truth of Christianity. They include such major controversies as the time of the rapture, the present existence of the "sign" spiritual gifts, perseverance of the saints, dispensationalism, or the variations in church worship and government.

So that we are not misunderstood here, we need to quickly add that discussions on such issues *are* still needed. It is important that we formulate our own views concerning them. Thus, sound teaching and preaching on these subjects is necessary. Pastors and other teachers should be clear about their own position, while pointing out that other believers hold alternate views. Just because these areas are not fundamental does *not* mean that they are unimportant or insignificant. This should help situations like Ken's above.

Since answers to secondary theological matters do not affect the truthfulness of the Christian faith, regardless of their outcome, differences on these subjects should not cause Christians to doubt. In other words, emotional quandaries should not result from topics that do not affect our eternal destiny. Not only should such differences not bother us, but we should actually *celebrate* them. It is nothing short of a great blessing to have the freedom in the body of Christ to hold divergent opinions on secondary matters. Differences of various sorts were present in the New Testament and are even more the case today. We should encourage believers to sit down with one another amicably, open up Scripture, and learn from each other. To share this common basis over a cup of coffee should be exhilarating.

Making such theological distinctions is crucial for our discussion of doubt. We must be able to give our attention to any number of theological matters, and enjoy doing it, but without causing any anxiety.

This is roughly what I explained to Ken that night he called. Once he distinguished primary from secondary doctrine, he recognized that his objections no longer had the force that he thought they did. So what if all evangelicals don't agree on all the specifics of secondary doctrine? Further, he realized that the firm basis for the fundamental doctrines, with at least four types of checks and balances, certainly disproved his claim that these beliefs were just a matter of interpretation. Ken was not only significantly relieved, but in the many conversations we've had in the ten years or so since that evening, he has never struggled again with this issue. Today, he just smiles and shakes his head when the subject comes up.

"Bad night," he quips. But that's the very heart of emotional doubt in a nutshell!

Conclusion

Kelly used to feel uncomfortable whenever her pastor prefaced a discussion by indicating that sincere Christians were divided over a certain issue. It especially troubled her when he explained that he just wanted to be honest about tough portions of Scripture. But she was relieved when, during a private conversation, he pointed out that none of these matters had any effect on the truthfulness of Christianity or her salvation. In fact, he explained how such an honest attitude allowed Christians to take a personal view on the doctrine, as well as actually being excited about the continuing opportunity to study the matter together.

Jarrod had a question about the doctrine of creation, which he rightly thought was one of Christianity's central tenets. Doing some research on the topic, he developed his own list of reasons for believing it. As a result, he was assured that this doctrine was both central and well evidenced.

Believers often experience doubt simply because they do not agree with each other concerning doctrinal issues that do not ultimately affect their faith either way, although these are still important areas of theology. We can live with questions like these, just as Christians did in the early church. Making distinctions like we have made here can keep us from unnecessary uncertainty and anxiety. Far from allowing difficult issues to cause us worry, this subject should actually encourage us in that God has allowed such freedom in the body of Christ.

10

Negative and Positive Consequences

Emotional doubt can lead to dire consequences, or it can help to produce believers who are vibrant and growing. It all depends on our response to it.

When Jennifer first called, she was a bit combative. Having read my earlier book on doubt (see bibliography), she wanted to argue about what kind of uncertainty she was experiencing. I listened to her description of the problem, then asked the same questions that we've discussed throughout this book.

"Don't tell me it's emotional," she responded.

"Why not?" I countered, sure that this was the nature of her unrest. "What would be wrong with that?"

"I just have an image in my mind of men in white coats," she answered.

It took a while to work through that misconception. Then, after realizing that I was probably correct in my identification, she issued her next challenge.

"And don't tell me to just pray and be spiritual. Everyone tells me that," she sputtered.

Over several lengthy phone calls, I understood more of where she was coming from. Fitting the description of the typical high-powered executive, Jennifer was a vice president in a large corporation. A good thinker with strong people-skills, she was moving quickly up the ladder. A single woman who was raised in a Christian family, she also possessed a fine grasp of Christian truth. But somehow her faith and her business practices were at odds with each other, and it was her faith that was suffering. She had prayed to trust Christ literally hundreds of times, but she still questioned her salvation so thoroughly that she didn't even consider herself to be a believer.

After many talks, including lengthy discussions about Philippians 4:6–9, she decided not to pursue a remedy for her doubt. She just wasn't ready to apply the procedure. "I'm going to let it go for a little while and see what happens," she reported.

About three years later, Jennifer called back. I was quite surprised to hear from her, given the way she had called off the earlier discussions. Over the years, she had moved from the West to the North, changed jobs, and, as judged by the business world, she was a raging success. But her private world was crumbling around her.

"My boss would think I was going nuts if he knew what I was calling about. He thinks I'm at the top of my career, but I'm completely miserable. What I want most, I can't have," she complained. "I don't care about money or success, I only want the Lord. But I don't think he wants me. It's affecting everything I do. I *have* to do something about it."

Jennifer's uncertainty had negatively affected every aspect of her life. She testified that not a day went by that it didn't cause her exceptional grief. When she began the second round of calls, she told me that she was at an all-time low point. She had a choice of either turning to the Lord or watching her life fall apart due to questioning her relationship with God. This time around, she did not even argue my identification of her struggles as emotional. She knew it to be the case.

Over the next few months we talked on a weekly basis. Jennifer's progress was slow, as she was exceptionally leery of applying the biblical steps or even admitting that they would be helpful at all. But once she began, she went at it tenaciously. Before too long, the walls of emotional doubt crumbled around her.

Jennifer developed into a textbook case of what can happen once the application of biblical principles takes place. In the ensuing months, she began to grow in her walk with the Lord. Having attended a biblical church all of her life, she had always been a worker and began leading a woman's Bible study, as well as talking to other women about their struggles with emotional doubt. In my twenty-five years of giving advice on this subject, seldom have I seen this drastic of a change. The Lord can do amazing things when people decide to get serious in the application of his principles!

We saw similar patterns in earlier chapters. Missy found that even suffering from a psychological disorder did not keep her from gaining victory over her need for assurance (chapter 8). James decided that the only way to conquer the severe childhood hurt in his life was to make the decision to apply biblical precepts (chapter 8). Ken's changed perspective on the nature of theology led to a corresponding modification of his views on Christianity as a whole (chapter 9). All three had changed from believers whose questioning dominated their lives to victorious, vibrant individuals. As the old saying goes, doubt can either make you or break you.

Negative Consequences

Throughout this book we have seen examples of changed lives that have come as a result of dealing with religious doubt. Yet, many of these people suffered significantly until they made the *decision* to change. We've also seen some cases where people chose not to do anything about their doubt, accepting those consequences, as well. In this chapter, we will look at five unfortunate consequences to which religious doubt can lead. While there may be some overlap here, each presents a different angle on the problem. Notice the progression between the stages of reaction. Doubt frequently moves similarly.

(1) **Doubt often leads to a degrading view of God.** The doubter almost always thinks that God has in some way abandoned him or her, or otherwise hurt them. After all, shouldn't God, who can do anything, want to help us feel better? Then why don't we have more peace, and less pain? In this line of questioning, it is surmised that God is at fault here. He must not care about me or want to help. This generally makes the emotional situation even worse, pushing the individual further from God and his truth.

Sadly, the bad theology keeps the sufferer from pursuing the truth: their own faulty thinking has produced this situation. As we have seen over and over again, our doubt arises, *not* from the circumstances around us, but from the things we tell ourselves *about* those circumstances. So not only is the doubter suffering, but he or she is likely compounding the uncertainty with bad thoughts about God.

(2) **Bad theology often encourages bad habits.** The murkiness moves further. Habits like thanklessness also develop. When children learn traits like this one, adults are quick to point out: "You kids would complain even if you got every last thing you wanted." Or, "Children are so ungrateful. I'd have been thankful if I'd gotten everything you have when I was small."

But as adults, are we any more thankful? We respond: "Well, that's different." How so? We are just as quick to blame God for all of our difficulties and even our shortcomings!

Cynicism develops, too. Once we've crossed the line to blaming God, *everything* can be laid at his doorstep. How convenient! We are no longer responsible for our thoughts and actions. God is supposed to kiss it and make it all better! If he doesn't do so, he's let us down. Sometimes we sneer at thoughts about him. But if an answer to prayer is sandwiched in there some place, God is a hero again. We can be such fickle people!

We could go on and continue to name more bad habits. But these are sufficient to make our point. Bad theology affects our attitudes. More seriously, sometimes there is no recovery from unthankfulness and especially cynicism. Once these attitudes are ingrained deeply into our psyches, it's hard to remove them. Have you ever decided to really not like someone and noticed what happens whenever you see them? Even when they're doing something positive, it's too late. Once we label someone a loser, it takes a lot to change that designation. It's just a short step to despising them. And when believers who suffer from this sort of doubt hear about God, they can begin to despise him, too, if they are not careful.

(3) **Bad theology and poor attitudes affect our motivation.** Why should people follow God when they think that he has wronged them? And what if he doesn't care about us at all? Does that make us want to follow him more?

When a believer loses his or her will to continue on the heavenly path, passivity sets in, like spiritual rigor mortis. Suffering a reversal of direction in our commitment to God can similarly be devastating. How do you get a dead person to move? There's a problem! It's so difficult to move what is no longer in motion toward a goal.

(4) Now we reach the flip side of apathy. **When we don't think and do the things we should, sometimes it's easier to do the things we shouldn't.** Sin always seems like an easier move. Sin is also contagious. One sin often leads to another. Once we've crossed the line and let our defenses down, it is so much easier to do it again. Most of us know the feeling that comes when, after losing weight and gaining most of it back again, we reach a place where we feel like we really don't care whether

or not we eat every cake and bowl of ice cream in the world! At that point, short of a major change of attitude and direction, we've lost the battle.

While passing through the area, Lee came to see me about her doubt. A college graduate and a believer, she was concerned about her motivation to follow the Lord. She determined that she was lagging in her commitment to the Lord due to the presence of regular sin in her life. But try as I might, she was no longer willing to turn to God. I will always remember the end of that last meeting, knowing that nothing had changed and that she would not repent and commit herself to him. It was a chilling departure.

(5) **The most serious of the repercussions of religious doubt comes to the one who seemingly abandons all or part of their faith and hardens their heart against the Lord.** Sometimes this comes as a result of a long struggle that started as factual questioning, moving on to emotional issues. Old wounds yield scars and perhaps a "Who cares?" attitude. It follows for many that if God isn't on their side, why should they have anything to do with him? This sort of believer has continued down his or her path and refused to benefit from all the many blessings of the Christian faith. Their decision comes in spite of all the evidences for faith, the emotional remedies provided by wonderfully healing texts like Philippians 4:6–9, and the possibility of victorious living in light of eternal life.

What are the possible signs that may indicate that someone is in this sort of danger? This is an exceptionally difficult question because we can never be sure of another's heart, or when someone has crossed the line. Neither should we presume to announce our opinions to or about such persons. But due to the seriousness of the situation, and out of sensitivity to our suffering brother or sister, we might still venture a humble, cautious response.

Perhaps the clearest indication is that the person is no longer thinking, acting, and talking in a biblical manner, or in keeping with their previous commitment. Maybe references to the Lord bring sneers or derogatory remarks. Or their own language about God may betray them—especially if it is flippant or callous. Another possible indication is the inability to make spiritual decisions. Like Israel, perhaps there is an insensitivity to spiritual things, as the writer of Hebrews warns (Heb. 3:1–15). Possibly there is a lack of fruit in their lives (Matt. 7:18–23; Heb. 6:7–8). They have probably abandoned Christian fellowship (Heb. 10:25).

What characteristics are necessary in the spiritual counselor? Sensitivity is absolutely required. The person must first be sensitive to the Lord, then to the hurting individual. The latter must never be given an excuse to think that we are responding for any reason other than out of love and concern for God, His Word, and them. Humility is also an essential. There must be absolutely no sign of haughtiness or arrogance, which are condemned by our Lord (Luke 18:9-14). Pray for discernment in these matters, for much may depend on the words of the adviser. Boldness may even be necessary here, if the situation demands it. The potential that a brother or sister in Christ may be in danger outweighs one's personal desire not to be involved in the situation.

How should the concerned person respond? What steps might be taken? Where do we begin? The best place to start is with ourselves. Spend time with the Lord in prayer. We need to search our own hearts in order to test our motives. Why are we getting involved? Is there any desire whatsoever just to meddle in someone else's life or see if we can uncover some tidbit about them? Do we feel like we "owe" them one? What about our own relationship to the Lord? Have we examined ourselves (1 Cor. 10:12; 11:31)? Have we repented of all known sins? As far as we know, is there anything between us and the Lord or between us and another believer?

Next, seek the advice of mature Christians. This is not a decision that should be made lightly, or by the judgment of a single individual.

Pray together and seek the Lord's will. Pray for the leading and intervention of the Holy Spirit. The work is his.

When meeting with the doubter, listen to his or her concerns. Ask good questions. Where are they now with the Lord? Be aware of any progression of the doubt. At what stage does it seem to be? Are they sensitive to the Lord? In what areas? How do they respond to the overall situation? Are they concerned? Remorseful? Where do they think their doubt might take them if they pursue their present course of action? Do you agree with their assessment? If necessary, be prepared to confront them lovingly, but firmly.

Some believers who are otherwise close to a serious problem may still respond, because of the work of the Holy Spirit. They may also be touched by your love and show of concern. If they are open to assistance, begin by suggesting repentance.

Then be prepared to suggest appropriate biblical steps that address the particular issue. We have made many such suggestions. Assist them in applying these principles or make immediate arrangements to do so. Regular follow-up and fellowship are also necessary.

Lest we give up hope on these individuals, however, let us remember the prodigal son—God is in the business of working miracles!

Steve was a college graduate, a very committed Christian, and a very intelligent young man who was well versed in philosophy and apologetics. But a few of his close friends told me that he had recently become an agnostic while finishing his Ph.D. I called Steve one night and asked him about his shift of allegiance. Imagine my surprise when he admitted that what I had heard about his agnosticism was true! We had several lengthy conversations, during which he admitted that the chief reason for his change was not factual, but a problem with sin. As is very common, he had concluded that those who would point out his problems were themselves the difficulty. It was almost as if he thought that rejecting his faith would still his conscience (and the conviction of the Holy Spirit).

While trying to speak in a compassionate manner, I was firm in my comments. I also addressed a few philosophical questions. Convicted, he eventually repented. Steve seemed serious about his return to the Lord. In fact, a few years later when we talked again, he was holding fast to his Christian faith.

Positive Consequences

Emotional doubt can also be the instigator that brings about positive results in the believer's life. We will list here seven of these advantageous side effects, some of which also overlap, in the hope that they will encourage doubters to both work on their uncertainty and continue to mature in their Christian walk, in spite of their questions.

(1) **We may learn how to study and discover answers for ourselves.** Especially with factual questions, few habits are more useful or gratifying. Some report that this is one of the most rewarding results of tangling with their religious quandaries. This knowledge should be helpful in future situations or in assisting others who have similar questions.

(2) **Having worked through uncertainty, we grow as whole persons.** Some researchers have even concluded that we do not grow as individuals unless we experience doubts and personally labor through various sorts of questions.

(3) **Thinking properly also teaches us to love the life that God has given to us.** Personal conflict helps us to appreciate existence without the problems. The only time pain feels good is when it subsides and finally stops. When we struggle with doubt, we value a life in which the questioning has calmed down enough so that we can stop and smell the roses.

(4) **We learn that our emotions are not evil or negative.** Contrary to the impression given by some researchers, emotions are not bad. They are God-given. Think of all the fantastic memories and other experiences

that are ours because of this wonderful gift from heaven. More than this, we have seen that these same emotions can be trained to behave! They can be brought into agreement with our thinking. Why not have the best of both gifts? This is a key emphasis in this book.

(5) **Working through emotional doubt helps us see it for what it is and properly identify it.** Some doubters talk about their doubt as an "It," a monster that grips them with fear at its every bidding. It chases and pursues them, scaring them almost to death. But additional reflection shows that this is certainly not the case. Rather than being some sort of ogre that sneaks up on us and attacks, our emotions are obviously part of us. Our feelings are like guard dogs, sitting by our side and watching out for us! They are not growling at us, but at the negative, unedifying thoughts that are approaching up the walkway towards us, as well as the ones we have already invited into our lives!

Emotions are spiritual alarm clocks, buzzing loudly when we are entertaining thoughts that we have no business contemplating. We may not like being awakened in the morning from a blissful sleep, but we're still happy for the availability of a wake-up call. This is what our emotions do for us. They are our alarm clock that sounds off when we cross the line into unedifying territory. We simply misinterpret its blessings, thinking we're being attacked! Chalk up one more misbelief on the subject.

Upon reflection, Terry discovered that her unwanted emotions were *not* evidence of her having "fallen away" from Christianity. Rather, she discovered that her feelings occurred precisely *because* she had entertained thoughts that were contrary to her Christian beliefs. So she decided to make the most of her passions. Learning to relax whenever the feelings popped up, she allowed her emotions to become an early warning system, sounding off whenever she began to think in a nonbiblical manner. This was her signal to begin one of the biblical strategies that she found so helpful. In so doing, the fear subsided substantially.

So the emotions that we thought were so negative have taken yet another ironic twist. Our feelings are on our side. They support our struggles. In a strange sort of way, God speaks to us through them!

(6) Not to miss the forest for the trees, **the experience of doubt can actually lead to its own death!** By dealing properly with our emotions, we can quiet at least the most painful side effects of such questioning, as well. Assurance and peace can actually be its conclusion (Phil. 4:7, 9). In other words, by learning to apply God's truth to our emotional struggles, our feelings can be trained. The application can be made in such a way that we learn to deal with all emotional matters, including emotional doubt, teaching us how to manage our most trying times in life.

(7) Lastly, **doubt helps our faith to mature.** Our new thinking should contribute to a deeper spirituality. We should come away from these trying times of uncertainty with a deeper desire to come to know better the God whose truth we believe. In this sense, Christian growth is taking place.

Having grown in the midst of our suffering, thankfulness and praise to God are the natural results. We develop a new appreciation for how he works in our life. Just like Job, although we may have started out by questioning him, we may end up actually being a living example of just how God works such a process out. Paul calls us God's workmanship (Eph. 2:10) and adds that God will finish the work he has begun in us (Phil. 1:6). Being obedient through the process of doubt can aid in that development.

Dealing with emotional doubt has taken us to the practice of biblical disciplines like prayer, thanksgiving, praise, meditation, and personal study. In working through our questioning, we have probably pursued the path of increased spirituality without even realizing it. Now, the last thing we should do is stop this process of growth when our pain begins to subside. In fact, this is the very time we should be increasing our spiritual progress, not only as preventive therapy, but also as a means of continued growth. The resulting maturation should continue to push us in the direction of practicing the other Christian disciplines, too. If, with the psalmist, we desire God and long for him with all of our hearts, then we should seek him (Ps. 42:1–2) by pursuing those practices that can increase our intimacy and fellowship with him.

Some may now ask a great question that has perhaps been building throughout the book. Since religious doubt produces so many positive consequences, why do we emphasize corrective thinking and try to change the feelings?

Such healing is needed for at least three reasons. First, we have also seen that, perhaps because of the many surprises on this topic, believers draw many false conclusions. But failing to deal with doubt in the correct manner can also lead to serious harm. We would like to stop this sort of problem before it gets a chance to develop. Second, the emotional element is frequently so painful that the person at least feels a need for immediate treatment. It is normal for human beings to want to avoid pain, even if it produces some positive results. Third, the benefits that come from doubt generally come only after the uncertainty is treated. The blessings, then, are largely manifest only in retrospect.

Conclusion

Over a period of twenty-five years, I have dealt with approximately one hundred cases of doubting individuals, both male and female, keeping records on almost every one of them. The vast majority of their problems (about three-quarters), were emotional in nature. I have had long-term follow-up contacts over the years with most of these people, the vast majority of whom improved significantly. Almost without exception, the emotional doubters, in particular, reported marked improvement.

Still, some refused to follow biblical instructions. Rejecting God's warnings and failing to follow his recipe for peace, they continued in their pain and uncertainty. Often, they blamed God and/or their circumstances, when their chief problem was what they told themselves and how they responded to their difficulties. I suspect that unless they have changed their thinking, these individuals are still hurting.

Obviously, the choice of how doubt will affect our lives is ours to make. The outcome can be either negative or positive. This book was written in the hopes that each reader will find the tools needed to make the choice for healing, and follow it to a peace-filled conclusion!

11

Selected Bibliography

We are finished with the "meat" of this book. You can stop here if you wish. Hopefully you will have gathered some gems to apply to your own life, or for use with a friend who may be in pain and seeking answers.

But if you are interested in finding resources for further study, then read on. We have focused on a fairly narrow theme, limiting ourselves primarily to emotional doubt. Where applicable, we tried to touch the surface of certain important subjects in other pertinent areas, so I will suggest a number of writings that are relevant to several of these issues. Beyond emotional doubt, we have generally remarked on various other factual, volitional, and emotional matters. Along the way, we have also mentioned other helpful topics, like total commitment to Jesus Christ and the practice of the Christian disciplines. While I have repeatedly said that I am not a psychologist, some of these books are written by specialists in these areas and could be meaningful.

Each resource is followed by a brief explanation to help you find the right book within the category you've chosen. Most of the texts are rather introductory and can be read with little background knowledge. Some are a bit more advanced, especially in the "Factual Issues" section. But there are no technical treatises on the list. Far more specialized and advanced texts are certainly available, and can often be located in the bibliographies of the following books.

I. Doubt

Anderson, Lynn. *If I Really Believe, Why Do I Have These Doubts? Hope for Those Who Feel They Will Never Measure Up to Other Christians' Faith.* Minneapolis: Bethany House Publishers, 1992. A popular approach to Christian belief, feelings, and growing in faith.

Beck, James R. "Treatment of Spiritual Doubt Among Obsessing Evangelicals." *Journal of Psychology and Theology.* Volume 9, number 3. Fall, 1981. This journal article argues that there might be a close connection between obsessing and questions of assurance.

Guinness, Os. *Doubt* (formerly titled *In Two Minds*). Herts, England: Lion Publishing, 1976. In a classic, insightful treatment, the subject is divided into seven "families," making suggestions for healing.

Habermas, Gary. *Dealing With Doubt.* Chicago: Moody Press, 1990. Investigates and addresses three species of religious doubt (factual, emotional, and volitional), providing further theory and background for this present study.

McGrath, Alister E. *The Sunnier Side of Doubt.* Grand Rapids: Zondervan Publishing House, 1990. A general introduction to select aspects, including the value of doubt and some thoughts about how it helps us to grow in our Christian lives.

II. Factual Issues (Apologetics)

Corduan, Winfried. *No Doubt About It: The Case for Christianity.* Nashville: Broadman & Holman Publishers, 1997. Covers a wide scope of apologetic issues, both philosophical and historical.

Craig, William Lane. *Reasonable Faith: Christian Truth and Apologetics.* Wheaton: Crossway Books, 1994. Chiefly addresses reasons for the existence of God and historical issues pertaining to Jesus Christ.

Geisler, Norman L. *Christian Apologetics.* Grand Rapids: Baker Book House, 1976. Contains more on methodological and philosophical issues than most other volumes of this genre.

Geisler, Norman L. and Ron Brooks. *When Skeptics Ask: A Handbook of Christian Evidences.* Wheaton: Victor Books, 1990. A valuable and wide-ranging overview of key apologetic issues that specializes in pithy responses to dozens of commonly asked questions.

Habermas, Gary. *The Historical Jesus: Ancient Evidence for the Life of Christ.* Joplin, MO: College Press Publishing Company, 1996. Responds in detail to attacks on the orthodox view of the historical Jesus before building a case for Jesus' resurrection, in particular.

Habermas, Gary and Terry L. Miethe. *Why Believe? God Exists! Rethinking the Case for God and Christianity.* Joplin, MO: College Press Publishing Company, 1993. Addresses some of the philosophical, scientific, moral, and historical grounds for theism.

Hoover, A. J. *The Case for Christian Theism: An Introduction to Apologetics.* Grand Rapids: Baker Book House, 1976. An historian responds to many challenges to Christian theism, as well as providing evidences in favor of it.

McDowell, Josh. *Evidence that Demands a Verdict: Historical Evidences for the Christian Faith*. San Bernardino, CA: Here's Life Publishers, Inc., 1972. A popular and accessible treatment that concentrates on Scripture and Jesus Christ.

Moreland, J. P. *Scaling the Secular City: A Defense of Christianity*. Grand Rapids: Baker Book House, 1987. An especially strong presentation of the philosophical and scientific foundations for Christian theism that moves on to New Testament evidences.

Nash, Ronald H. *Faith and Reason: Searching for a Rational Faith*. Grand Rapids: Zondervan Publishing House, 1988. A presuppositional look especially at the philosophical basis undergirding Christianity.

Wilkins, Michael J. and J. P. Moreland, Editors. *Jesus Under Fire: Modern Scholarship Reinvents the Historical Jesus*. Grand Rapids: Zondervan Publishing House, 1995. Several scholars defend the Jesus of the New Testament, especially against the claims of the Jesus Seminar.

III. Emotional Issues

Backus, William. *Telling the Truth to Troubled People*. Minneapolis: Bethany House Publishers, 1985. A handbook to assist Christian counselors in applying Misbelief Therapy to hurting people.

_____. *The Good News about Worry*. Minneapolis: Bethany House Publishers, 1991. The application of Misbelief Therapy and other methods to various forms of anxiety.

Backus, William and Marie Chapian. *Telling Yourself the Truth*. Minneapolis: Bethany House Publishers, 1980. Arguably the best of the general applications of truth to the misbeliefs that Christians tell themselves.

Cloud, Henry and John Townsend. *False Assumptions.* Grand Rapids: Zondervan Publishing House, 1994. Exposes twelve false assumptions in the Christian's life that can lead to painful consequences.

Craig, William Lane. *No Easy Answers.* Chicago: Moody Press, 1990. Directed to common emotional (and other) questions about faith.

Lewis, C. S. "Religion: Reality or Substitute?" *Christian Reflections.* Edited by Walter Hooper. Grand Rapids: William B. Eerdmans Publishing Company, 1967. Perhaps the best and most insightful brief assessment of the effect that our emotions can have on our faith.

McGee, Robert S. *The Search for Significance.* Houston: Rapha Publishing, 1987. Exposes unbiblical attempts to anchor self-worth, including exercises to test one's present responses.

Thurman, Chris. *The Lies We Believe.* Nashville: Thomas Nelson Publishers, 1989. Investigates in detail false beliefs in five major areas, including providing numerous truths to combat each.

IV. Volitional Issues

Backus, William. *Finding the Freedom of Self-Control.* Minneapolis: Bethany House Publishers, 1987. Applies Misbelief Therapy to breaking bad habits in several areas.

Backus, William and Marie Chapian. *Why Do I Do What I Don't Want to Do?* Minneapolis: Bethany House Publishers, 1984. A manual written to help break the bondage of temptation and sin.

Kreeft, Peter. *Heaven: The Heart's Deepest Longing.* San Francisco: Harper and Row Publishers, 1980. An incredibly insightful book on eternal life being the preeminent desire of human beings.

Lewis, C. S. "On Obstinacy in Belief." *The World's Last Night and Other Essays*. New York: Harcourt, Brace, Jovanovich, 1960. Compelling writing that explains why Christians should stay faithful to Jesus Christ even when we do not always understand the whys and wherefores of our belief.

_____. "The Weight of Glory." *The Weight of Glory and Other Addresses*. Grand Rapids: William B. Eerdmans Publishing Company, 1949. A famous and inspirational sermon on the desire for eternity.

Piper, John. *Desiring God: Meditations of a Christian Hedonist*. Portland, OR: Multnomah Books, 1986. A study of Christian motivation that calls believers to seek godly pleasures.

V. Theological Differences

Mayers, Ronald B. *Evangelical Perspectives: Toward a Biblical Balance*. Lanham, MD: University Press of America, 1987. A plea to preserve orthodox theology and doctrinal maturity with a careful balance being given to biblical distinctives.

Parkinson, Joel R. *Orthodoxy and Heresy: Where to Draw the Line*. Shippensburg, Penn.: Companion Press, 1991. Contrasts the content of orthodox Christianity with heretical views and draws practical conclusions.

VI. Christian Commitment and the Christian Disciplines

Bonhoeffer, Dietrich. *The Cost of Discipleship*. Translated by R. H. Fuller. New York: The Macmillan Company, 1959. A classic treatment of being surrendered to Jesus Christ, making him the prominent person in our lives.

Foster, Richard J. *Celebration of Discipline: The Path to Spiritual Growth.* Revised Edition. San Francisco: Harper and Row, 1988. An introduction to the practice of about a dozen disciplines for the Christian life.

_____. *Freedom of Simplicity.* San Francisco: Harper and Row, Publishers, 1981. The biblical basis and present practice of the concept of directing our lives singlemindedly towards God.

_____. *Prayer: Finding the Heart's True Home.* San Francisco: Harper San Francisco, 1992. The identity and practice of more than twenty varieties of prayer.

Habermas, Gary R. "Meditation: A Forgotten Discipline." *Northwest Evangelical Baptist Journal,* Volume 3, Number 1. June, 1993. The identification, biblical basis, and practice of Christian meditation.

MacDonald, George. *True Discipleship.* Kansas City, KS: Walterick Publishers, 1976. A challenging summons to apply biblical teachings regarding living a life of total commitment to Jesus Christ.

Verwer, George. *Come! Live! Die! The Real Revolution.* Wheaton: Tyndale House Publishers, 1972. A call to Christians to dare to be sold out to God in every aspect of their lives.

Willard, Dallas. *The Spirit of the Disciplines: Understanding How God Changes Lives.* San Francisco: Harper and Row, Publishers, 1988. A theology of the disciplines that argues that believers can become more Christlike through the practice of imitating his life.

About the Author

Gary R. Habermas is Distinguished Professor of Apologetics and Philosophy and Chair of the Department of Philosophy and Theology at Liberty University, Lynchburg, Virginia. He has authored, co-authored, or edited twenty-two books, including his debate with Antony Flew, *Did Jesus Rise from the Dead?* (Harper and Row), *The Resurrection of Jesus* (Baker), with J. P. Moreland, *Beyond Death* (Crossway), and co-edited with Doug Geivett, *Miracles* (InterVarsity). He received his Ph.D. from Michigan State University and a D.D. from Emmanuel College, Oxford, England. He has also published more than one hundred articles of various sorts. He lives in Lynchburg with his wife Eileen and three of their seven children.